DRINK

DRINK

CONSTANTINE FITZGIBBON

Foreword by
Professor J. N. P. Moore, MD, FRCPI, DPM

GRANADA
London Toronto Sydney New York

Granada Publishing Limited
Frogmore, St Albans, Herts AL2 2NF
and
3 Upper James Street, London W1R 4BP
866 United Nations Plaza, New York, NY 10017, USA
117 York Street, Sydney, NSW 2000, Australia
100 Skyway Avenue, Rexdale, Ontario M9W 3A6, Canada
PO Box 84165, Greenside, 2034 Johannesburg, South Africa
CML Centre, Queen & Wyndham Streets, Auckland 1, New Zealand

Published by Granada Publishing 1980

Copyright © 1980 Constantine FitzGibbon

ISBN 0 246 10966 1

Printed in Great Britain by Richard Clay (The Chaucer Press) Ltd,
Bungay, Suffolk

Granada ®
Granada Publishing ®

This book is dedicated to the memory of many dead friends, but above all to that of my sister

MIMI

Vaya con Dios.

FOREWORD

by

Professor J. N. P. Moore, M.D., F.R.C.P.I., F.R.C. PSYCH., D.P.M.

To those accustomed to reading the pedestrian prose of the average contributor to medical and scientific journals, it is a pleasure and, therefore, additionally profitable to read a familiar subject discussed by a professional writer. Constantine FitzGibbon's words flow freely from his pen, and his frequent literary allusions and topical anecdotes tease the memory and stimulate reflection.

Throughout the ages man has sought to modify the harsh realities of his environment as well as the inevitable disappointments and frustrations of daily life by the use of tranquilizing agents. Some reflective and enlightened sages have sought to expand consciousness and transcend the constraints and frailties of the human condition by means such as meditation, techniques of physical and mental relaxation, devotional exercises or religious experiences. The discipline and dedication demanded by such methods seem possible only to those spiritually minded people with a philosophical bent, or simpler folk who undergo the fascinating but inexplicable phenomenon of conversion to a faith. For them it appears possible to rise above the limitations of human physiology and, indeed, anatomy. Life takes on new dimensions, energy seems liberated, fatigue diminished, and emotional life enriched. In such states "the slings and arrows of outrageous fortune" seem countered by an enviable serenity.

Alas, it is easier to dull consciousness than expand it, and human ingenuity has found many ways of doing so. Different ages and different races have found varied means of achieving chemically induced tranquillity. With the aid of drugs, senses are muted, physical discomforts are minimized, carking doubts and fears diminished, and a transient, if spurious, sense of liberation is experienced. In his early chapters Mr. FitzGibbon recounts with erudition some of these methods, and the gradual evolution of ethyl alcohol as the dominant tranquilizing drug of Western society.

Another fascinating aspect of this story of man's efforts to modify his reactions to reality is the apparent inevitability of excesses, whether these be the extremes of the contemplative religious fanatic, the histrionics of the revivalist movements, or the boisterous and often anti-social behavior of the inebriated. More sinister is the physical and mental deterioration, the inevitable consequences of the continuous excessive use of chemical agents, whether alcohol or other drugs. Sometimes it is the quantity of the drug which damages: sometimes it appears to be the vulnerability of the individual which leads to disaster. Thus, throughout history, efforts to reap the pleasures and profits of the controlled use of these anodynes, as well as to mitigate the painful effects of their misuse, have been an inevitable feature of succeeding generations. The story of these attempts at prevention, from precept to prohibition, makes fascinating reading.

A recital of the scientific or clinical details of any illness can be dull reading to any but the interested professional; and, indeed, discussion of the drama of any sickness or operation is one of the better known and more uninteresting items in the repertoire of the traditional club bore. It is, thus, a triumph of the writer's art that this book, which is primarily biographical and anecdotal rather than scientific or statistical, holds the attention from start to finish.

It is always intriguing when a well-known personage makes a public confession. In this case it is the story of the gradually developing insight and realization by the author that his drinking has taken on the characteristics of a progressive disease. Progress from outright rejection of the idea through rationalization and projection on his environment to final acceptance is faithfully and dramatically recorded. The somewhat discursive style, with numerous asides and details of his personal life and relationships, is a subtle way of sugaring the pill and getting home the realities of a deteriorating illness.

The relationship between mood changes, especially depression and problem drinking, is well portrayed. The physical well-being and zest for life which have so clearly followed acceptance of the inevitable, prove once again that when alcohol has become a need it has also become an enemy. Giving it up is not denial, but liberation.

This story of a personal emancipation will dispel for many people the mythology and comforting clichés which surround the drinking habits of the Western world. The book brings together much diverse and unusual as well as better known facts about the disease, alcoholism. Reading it will be an educational experience for many people—writing it represents a courageous act on the part of Constantine FitzGibbon.

ACKNOWLEDGMENTS

My debt of gratitude to Professor J. N. P. Moore, M.D., F.R.C.P.I., D.P.M. is very great indeed. Not only did he help steer my thinking concerning the medical matters here under discussion, but he corrected the first draft most thoroughly as well as advising me where I could best find the material I needed. For any lacunae that may remain I alone am, of course, responsible. Finally, he did me the great honor of writing the Foreword.

I should also like to acknowledge the help of Colonel Adams, of the Irish National Council on Alcoholism, for his help in providing me with factual and statistical information, and to Dr. David Thomas, who has been my doctor for some twelve years and who gave me, from his files and memory, a medical history of my own alcoholism during that period.

I also wish to thank Dr. John Cooney, M.B., M.R.C. Psych., D. Ch., Ph.D., who has not only taught me much but has cared for my wife consistently, and less so for myself, during these same twelve years. Much of what is contained in this book derives from his teaching and practice.

My wife, Marjorie, has allowed me to draw without hindrance or marital censorship on her own experiences as an alcoholic. I do not need to thank her here. On the other hand I should like to thank Mrs. George Morrison ("Theodora FitzGibbon") for information concerning my own drinking during the fifteen years that she was married to me.

As a final expression of gratitude I should like to thank, personally, Mr. Ken McCormick, of Messrs. Doubleday and Company, Inc., who not only encouraged me, as an old friend, to write this book but who also, through Doubleday, gave me the financial means to do so. I suspect that many writers owe more to a good publisher than is usually revealed.

Many reformed alcoholics have helped me with personal experiences. I am sure that they prefer to remain anonymous.

CONTENTS

CHAPTER I

Beginnings

This is a book about alcoholism, written by an alcoholic. It is not an autobiography, since my sixty-odd years have contained much more than my alcoholism. On the other hand a great deal is about myself, rather less about my present wife, who is also an alcoholic. But again her life, like my own, has only in part been dominated by drink, for she was a well-known actress before she became a well-known painter and sculptor. If I write so much about her, and even more about myself, it is as "case histories," the two case histories best known to me, and indeed I write about Marjorie almost entirely in relationship to myself.

Many of my close friends were or are alcoholics. If I write "were" it is not because they were cured of the disease—there is no known cure—but because they are dead. Only one of these have I attempted, not here, to study in depth. I was Dylan Thomas's official biographer and I also edited his letters. I did not dwell on his drinking habits because I certainly did not, and do not, regard those as his most interesting and important activity, though other writers appear to have done so. On the other hand, had he stopped drinking he would probably still be alive and the literature of the English-speaking peoples enriched by twenty-five years of his unwritten work. Had I not stopped drinking I might myself have been dead by now, and certainly this book would never have existed.

I am not a doctor, let alone a psychiatrist. Only in the preparation of this book have I attempted to study a medical subject and have discovered that in this field the doctors not only disagree but are also, on occasion, wildly and simply wrong. And they are dealing with a psychosomatic malady which perhaps

causes more misery than any other form of sickness, for each alcoholic affects not only himself or herself but virtually all
those persons with whom he or she is in close emotional or social
or economic contact. My knowledge of psychology is perhaps
about that of the average educated man, to which must be
added the fact that I am also a novelist.

But it is primarily because I am an alcoholic that I am capable
of writing about the subject. I therefore propose to arrange my
material as follows: first I shall describe, quite briefly, my inher-
itance (for heredity is highly relevant to many alcoholics), my
formative years as a child insofar as these concern later developments, up to what is technically called the prodromal phase of
my drinking. This prodromal phase is in effect a phase through
which all drinkers pass and in which even the great majority of
heavy drinkers remain. With me it lasted until about the ages of
twenty-six to thirty. It is the last stage at which the descent into
alcoholism may be halted without the total abandonment of
drink. I shall then devote a hundred or so pages to the nature of
alcoholism, its treatment or maltreatment, and the many failed
attempts to control or prevent it by medicine, by the churches,
by the law, and so on.

I shall return to my own story as it has unfolded over the past
thirty years, to the excuses I made and the lies I told both to myself and to others, and to even more unpleasant experiences
through which I passed, through which in differing circumstances and to varying degrees all alcoholics pass.

I shall end with the treatment that enabled me to stop drinking. Perhaps the most important, and certainly the most difficult,
part of this treatment is the first step which every alcoholic can
take only in the utter solitude of the condemned cell to which he
has been consigned: the acceptance of his condition. This must
precede his determination to be released from that cell. Then, in
almost all cases, help is needed, both expert medical help (which
at present, sadly, few doctors can provide) and, perhaps even
more important, help from those whom the alcoholic loves and
respects and who have managed to retain their love and respect
for him. If, in his miserable condition, he has driven all away, he
can perhaps find a surrogate in the companionship of other

reformed alcoholics, who will at least understand while he sets about the long process of rebuilding his life in freedom.

My family's motto is *Dum Spiro Spero,* "While there is breath there is hope." This is perhaps more true of the alcoholic, and of those close to him or her, than of any other sort of prisoner, any other sort of invalid. It is really in an attempt to convey that message that this book is written.

Since each individual is, by definition, different from all others, and since this is in no way otherwise with alcoholics, the textbooks tend to be misleading or at least unconvincing in their descriptions of alcoholic progress. Yet all that is known for certain about the disease in its early stages is the similarity of symptoms, but not all of these are present in every embryonic alcoholic and their variation of intensity is very great. Furthermore, environment must play a far greater part in the development of alcoholism—even if we tentatively dismiss the claim that it is the sole cause—than it does in, say, cancer of the throat. Thus the attempts of the textbooks to produce an average alcoholic end in the creation of a drunken tailor's dummy, a middle-class office worker with a wife and children and a fondness for drink. The female alcoholic, in the textbooks, comes of the same social milieu, is "a housewife" with or without children, and has no interests other than the bottle. That there are such people I have no doubt, only I have never met them.

In her well-known *Primer on Alcoholism* Mrs. Marty Mann attempts to give her picture of alcoholics more flesh and blood by quoting or inventing a dozen or so case histories. However, these are so brief that she would require the pen of a Chekhov or a Maupassant (or the scope of a Dostoevsky) to breathe life into them, and these she lacks. Indeed, the three best modern books about an alcoholic are written by three of the finest writers of their generation, all themselves alcoholics and all now dead. These are: *Under the Volcano* by Malcolm Lowry; *The Lost Weekend,* by Charles Jackson; and passages in the books of F. Scott Fitzgerald, in particular *The Crack-up.* To these must be added another, more "specialized" study of alcoholic paranoia, again by a very fine writer, Evelyn Waugh's *The Ordeal of Gilbert Pinfold.* I know of no book by a woman writer that deals with the subject in any other than superficial terms, though a certain amount can be learned from the first volume of autobiography written by Nina Hamnett, *Laughing Torso.*

It is not my intention here to write autobiography, but it seems to me only fair to the reader that he or she have a skeleton outline of what I was doing and drinking during my life. Some of this I have already published elsewhere, but I shall avoid the commercial temptation of referring the reader to other books of mine, most of which are in any case out of print.

Heredity   My father was an Irishman, of aristocratic Norman-Irish ancestry. For three or four generations he came of a line of what Bernard Shaw once called down-starts. He was born about 1887 and trained for the Royal Navy, but gave this up to make a living as a cotton broker in New York. He did extremely well, when first married to my mother, and they lived in Tuxedo Park and moved in the highest society. It was a hard-drinking society and my late mother told me that my father had a quite astonishingly strong head. She never saw him the worse for drink, even after an all-night poker party when the other men were showing definite signs of it.

In 1914 he rejoined the Royal Navy, in which he served with some distinction throughout the war. Either just before or during the war he took to drugs. By the time the war was over he was a fully fledged drug addict and his discharge from the Navy seems to have been not unconnected with this. My mother understood nothing whatsoever about drugs, but was aware that he was running rapidly through the limited fortune she had inherited from her father. She said that at one time he was sniffing ether, and that it was this disgusting smell which made her seek advice. A doctor told her that he was taking enough drugs, of all sorts, theoretically to kill eight men, and that he was incurable. Her friends advised her to divorce him, if only for the sake of her four children. (I was the youngest, with three older sisters.) She loved him deeply, indeed at the end of her life she told me that he was the only man she had ever really loved. Reluctantly she divorced him, when I was about two. I saw him only very occasionally before I was grown up, and my mother never spoke of him save in vague and friendly terms. He therefore had no direct personal influence on me.

I learned about his doping when I was thirteen. At Wellington, a predominantly military school, my housemaster sent for me and told me that my father had been sent to prison, on check offenses. I was unmoved. He was later sent to prison a second time, for similar offenses, and was there cured of the dope habit. From 1941 until the end of the war my mother put him up at her house in England. (He had meanwhile been married and divorced again.) I got to know him when I was on leave and after the war, when he was living in the house of his sister, my aunt, also in England. He drank a little, perhaps two or three whiskeys a day at the most, but he never took drugs again. I rather liked him, as a friend, and felt pity rather than resentment for him. He was a witty man and good company. He never showed or, I suspect, felt the slightest shame for anything he had ever done, nor any trace of self-pity. This absence of shame or guilt I have inherited from him. I have never been to prison but expect that if I had been, or do go, I should joke about it as he did. As I say, he had no direct influence on me in my childhood, or after I grew up. But I both hate and fear drugs, which, for obvious subjective reasons, I cannot emotionally equate even now with alcohol, though I tell myself that objectively there is little to choose between them.

His father, my grandfather, I never knew, since he died before my birth. He had spent what money he had early on and apparently never attempted to earn any more, apart from a brief period as a soldier. I believe he fought in the Crimean War. He retired to Dinard in France, which is where my American mother met the family. His wife supported him, it seems, by making hats. He himself stayed in bed all day, getting up in the evening and drinking whiskey, alone, all night. I have heard that his wife, my grandmother, who was also dead when I was born, used to water the whiskey. So did he, to conceal how much he had drunk. Within a few days the decanter was crystal clear and had to be emptied. My mother has told me that when he did surface he was most witty and amusing, but very vague. She said that there was no malice in him, as there was none in my father, nor I hope in me.

My great-grandmother, Lady Louisa FitzGibbon, was heiress to a large property in the County Limerick. She married a younger son of the Lord Dillon of the time. He took her name. She appears to have been a great gambler, as was my father. She lost the estate, the great house, and all its contents in the 1880s. The house was burned, when empty, by the I.R.A. in 1920. Its ruin is still extremely impressive.

My mother's family history was very different. Née Folsom, she gave birth to me in my grandfather's house in Lenox, Massachusetts. He had been very rich but had been swindled by his business partner or man-of-affairs out of a substantial part of his fortune. His money came from New York, Stuyvesant money, for he was descended both from Peter Stuyvesant and also from John Winthrop, the first effective governor of the Massachusetts Bay Colony. Both his father and his grandfather had been American Minister at The Hague. He himself was a close friend of Grover Cleveland, but took no part in public life. He was a painter of some talent and a photographer of more. I never knew him, but he seems to have been an extremely upright man in the very best early American tradition. His wife, my grandmother, I just remember. She was a Fuller, from Vermont. They were not rich, but were talented. Margaret Fuller, the writer and early feminist, was her aunt. A sister married Whistler's brother. Her grandfather, Timothy Fuller, had played a not very significant part in the American Revolution or the drafting of the Constitution, I forget which. My mother was no sort of a snob and despised snobbery in others. If I have inherited an addiction to drink and a certain genealogical pride, it is not from that side of my family.

Not that my mother was in any way opposed to drink. She drank, in moderation, all her life. Shortly before her death she wrote to me that she now had nothing left to live for. She had lost the use of her eyes, and so could no longer read. She had, she said, even lost any pleasure in her evening scotch and soda. She was not a religious woman, nor any sort of moralist, but she did have some belief in God. Her mother was a Unitarian, and I remember amusing her by telling her that Unitarians are said to believe in one God, at most. We discussed my drinking, particularly after my youngest sister had died of it at the age of forty. She never reproached me, but she asked me not to drive a car. I took this to be a promise, which I have kept. I believe that such artistic talents as I possess I have inherited from that side of my family, such addictive qualities from my father's.

Childhood We lived in America until I was eight, that is to say until 1927, our home being New York, where my mother worked. Our holidays were spent in Lenox, where for at least one term I attended the village school. One of my earliest memories is of my youngest sister, Mimi, mixing dry martinis for my mother's guests at 186 East Seventy-fifth Street. I do not recall ever seeing a drunken man or woman during my childhood. I never saw my mother in any way the worse for drink.

In 1927 my mother married a very distant cousin, Bertram Winthrop. He was an international lawyer, really more French than American, and we moved to Paris. During that brief marriage, for they were divorced in 1931, Bertram played very little part in my life. He was certainly no sort of a substitute father figure to me, though always kind and considerate. He was a most distinguished lawyer—he had been one of President Wilson's legal advisers during the Peace Treaty negotiations—and a sober, upright man. He was also very rich, and my mother extracted far less alimony from him than she could have done. I was sent to boarding school in England in 1928, to the New Beacon, where I was, I think, as happy as a schoolboy can be. My sisters were also at English boarding schools, the eldest at Oxford. I had no trouble with my schooling, being invariably top of my class in all subjects and sailing through the examinations.

In 1931 my mother, divorced now, bought a house in Devonshire. We were no longer very rich, but were certainly not poor.

Meanwhile I had got drunk for the first time. It was really an infantile accident and had happened at St. Moritz, during the Christmas holidays of 1930–31, where we had been lent a house. I had been left alone one evening and had discovered a bottle of cherry brandy. It smelled, and then tasted, delicious, and I drank the lot. I was unconscious on the pantry floor when my mother and sisters arrived home. Incidentally, I had been drinking watered wine with my meals when on holiday in France.

Early Depressions More important, perhaps, I had experienced in St. Moritz the first deep depression that I can recall. I was alone a great deal, for we knew no children of my age, and though I skated and skied, I did so on my own. It was before sleeping that I felt this depression. It took a visual form. All would be white before my closed eyes, comprehensible enough in St. Moritz, but this white would suddenly change to a hideous patternless mixture of mud and dirty greens and black, and this made me very unhappy. This may have been prepubertal tension, or it may have been an early manifestation of endogenous depression, a term that will be explained later.

In 1932 I sat for a scholarship examination for Wellington. I won a nomination, which was a sort of second-rate scholarship, carrying some money with it. The headmaster of the New Beacon did not wish me to take it, since the Wellington exam had been intended as a trial run for the Eton scholarship in the following term. But my mother was beginning to worry about money. She always did, for she had little idea of how to handle her affairs and was, quite unnecessarily, paying income tax both in England and America. So she decided I should go to Wellington with this wretched nomination. I did so, in January of 1933. I always disliked the place, with its silly emphasis on sport, though as usual I had no trouble with my studies.

A curious incident of about 1932 or 1933 may be relevant. My father came down to Devonshire specifically to see me. My mother told me of this, and I hid in the woods until he was gone, thus not seeing him at all. Perhaps more curious, I had no recollection of this experience at all until my mother told me of it, thirty years later.

End of Childhood   The summer of 1934 we spent in Lenox. I traveled over alone, third class on some liner, and, I remember, read all of Pepys, which I had won as a school prize. I had that summer taken my school certificate and had won honors in eight subjects, which I believe was some sort of record either for age or for the number of honors or both.

Lenox was freedom and bliss. A dozen families had children of my age, and indeed the whole of our little society was like one big family. I caddied at the golf club for pocket money (once for Al Smith) and tips were generous. I fell in love with almost all the girls. Prohibition had recently been repealed, and at night we would drive out, to a place called The Log Cabin, and drink planter's punch, a strong, sweet concoction based on rum. We went to dances at the Lenox Club and elsewhere, with hip flasks. I think it was then that my mother asked me not to drive. I also recall hangovers, which I associate with solitary depression.

I returned to Wellington, with its dreary football and to me equally dreary homosexuality, which I tried but did not like. On the rare occasions when we were allowed out I would bicycle as far as I could with a friend and we would drink beer and discuss rebellion. I rebelled against everything that Wellington stood for and in the spring of 1935 the authorities asked my mother to take me away from the school.

She asked me what I should like to do. I was not quite sixteen, and I said I should like to go to Germany and learn German. (I was already bilingual in French.) I went to Berlin, with an allowance of three pounds per week until the age of twenty-one. This I spent on books and on beer, in that order. It cannot have been much beer, though the family with whom I lived gave me a bottle with my evening meal. Cigarettes I rationed to three a day. I liked Berlin and spent a great deal of time in the museums and art galleries. I also lost my virginity, to a model girl who had taken a fancy to me and who indeed wrote to me the other day.

I decided to go to Munich and study painting. I went first to a family but later to the Students' Hostel. I attended an art school, but rapidly discovered that I could not draw. So I wrote to my mother, who had now sold the Devonshire house, and was living between London, Jersey (to avoid English taxation), and America, that I wished to go to Oxford. She replied that I could hardly do that on three pounds a week, and that I had better win a scholarship.

For a year and a half I lived between Munich, where I attended the university, and Paris, where I was also an extramural student at the Sorbonne. I was given guidelines by Dr. Marrett, the Rector of Exeter College, whom I had met when visiting my mother on Jersey. I read prodigiously, in Germany Goethe primarily, in France poetry, particularly the *symbolistes* and above all Rimbaud. I spent one summer term at Angers Univer-

sity, reviving my Latin and attending lectures on French literature and history. I lodged in a seminary, where I was the only
boy or young man not destined for the priesthood. Its head, the
Chanoine de Civray, took a liking to me and gave me special
tuition. And in December of 1936 I won an open modern lan-
guages scholarship to Oxford.

During my time in Paris I had come to know a surprisingly
large number of writers, some famous, such as Cocteau and
Montherlant, many less so. I was, I suppose, remarkably grown
up for my age and almost totally international. I drank in the
cafés of the period, the Flore and the Dôme, and there acquired
a great deal of adult knowledge. I could not of course drink
much on three pounds a week, and my love affairs were brief
and transitory. Also I worked very hard. I recall Parisian nights,
in my little room, pushing aside my books and listening to the
great city with a longing for the lights and the music and the
talk and the beautiful women, but my three pounds was exhausted. That is the nearest I came to depression during this
period of my life, which was also when I decided that I should
one day be a writer.

In London, after I had won my scholarship, there was a ten
months' hiatus before I began my first term at Oxford. I had a
room in Oakley Street, Chelsea, and it is there that I first recall
willfully getting drunk. This was quite deliberate: I wanted
to know what it was like. So I went to Dakin's, the grocer on the
corner, and bought three bottles of the cheapest red wine. I
drank these, while reading Jules Romains' *Hommes de bonne
volonté*, until the print swirled before my eyes and the room
began to revolve. This did not seem to me particularly interesting or pleasant, the wine had not tasted very good, and next
morning I had a headache and a dry mouth.

What I looked for in London and soon found were pubs
equivalent to the Flore and the Dôme, to Montparnasse and
Saint-Germain-des-Prés. Chelsea had a reputation as an "artistic"
quarter, but this was well out of date, although a few writers and
painters lived there. Those visible in the Chelsea pubs, of which
the Six Bells was the most famous, were usually old and often
dressed in the grotesque artistic fashion of the nineties, with

capes, beards, and huge tam-o'-shanters. Even the generation before mine, the generation of T. S. Eliot and Henry Moore, had cast aside such fancy-dress. Writers and painters now dressed just like anybody else, with perhaps a slight proletarian tinge, intended to indicate left-wing sympathies, for in those days "we" were all left-wing and frequently called ourselves, as I had done at Wellington, communists.

So far as we were concerned Bloomsbury had followed the Yellow Book generation into oblivion, though many of its most distinguished members, Virginia Woolf, Clive Bell, Bertrand Russell, Duncan Grant, and others, were in fact very much alive. They had little interest for us, nor presumably we for them. The pubs for us, in the late thirties, were in the Charlotte Street area, which I have sometimes seen called Fitzrovia but which we called Soho: the Fitzroy, the Marquis of Granby, and above all the Wheatsheaf. Through the Wheatsheaf, at that time, passed almost all the young men and women who have since become famous in the arts, and a great many who have not. There were plenty of girls, too, young actresses and models. The place was crowded, but conversation does not seem to have been difficult. We drank beer and invented the arts. We were poor, but we drank as much as we could afford. And when the Wheatsheaf closed we usually had an extra hour of drinking in the cheap part of the Café Royal, with a property sandwich that made our beer legally a meal. It was in the Wheatsheaf, the Dôme, and the Flore that I made my first, now my oldest, friends. And it was then that I learned to believe that drink and art go hand in hand.

I spent part of that summer with a girl friend in the South of France, and had the traumatic experience of her pregnancy, which I refer to again later. I also acted with her in the little summer theater at Shere, in a surrealist translation of a play written by, I think, Euripides. (I leave the reader to work that one out.) I contributed to one or two small magazines. I drank a lot of beer and, when I could afford it, Canadian Club whiskey. In October I went up to Oxford.

Early Manhood I arrived at Oxford late, drunk—my youngest sister had been married that day—without my luggage but with a large nude painting of my girl under my arm. I certainly had not

come up to Oxford in order to learn how to drink like a gentle-
man.

I did very little work at Oxford, and drank far too much—on
credit. I grew increasingly depressed, until in March of 1939 I
felt so suicidal that I asked to see a doctor. His diagnosis was
that I needed more exercise, mine that my depression was due
to the coming war, in which I should presumably be killed, and
that I wanted to leave Oxford and enjoy myself (which meant
drink, girls, and editing a small magazine, also on credit). In retrospect I am sure that my depression and general misery that
spring were caused, in part, by the political situation, in part by
my poverty. I assume that my continued heavy drinking was an
attempt to counteract that depression, but that in fact it had precisely the contrary effect, such as is described in *Medical Aspects
of Alcoholism* (Dublin, undated but after 1973) as Part Two of
the prealcoholic symptomatic phase "constant relief drinking
which becomes a mode of drinking". I was also developing a
strong head, which is described as Part Three of that phase. I
left Oxford in the spring of 1939.

However, for a further year my life continued much as before.
I volunteered for the Royal Air Force on September 3, 1939, but
in fact ended up in the Army in early June 1940. During most of
this time I did nothing, awaiting my call-up and failing eyesight
tests for the Royal Air Force and the Fleet Air Arm, though for a
few weeks I had an office job in the City of London. I was living
with another girl, having even been very briefly married to yet a
third. Our life was much as I had made it: the Wheatsheaf and
other pubs, association almost exclusively with people connected
with the arts and who drank much as I did, poverty and debt
(but no Oxford tradesmen now), and bouts of depression. That
winter of the phony war was a period of great strain for all, and
many of us were delighted when it ended, even well nigh cata-
strophically, in May 1940. I simply went to a recruiting center
and enlisted in the Irish Guards. A couple of weeks later I arrived, penniless, at the Guards Depot, Caterham. This was two
days before my twenty-first birthday. My fellow recruits in my
squad bought me a few glasses of Guinness in the canteen called
the NAAFI. And, true to her word, my mother ended my allow-

ance. She must have been getting a bit tired of me—who can blame her?—for to the best of my recollection she did not send me a birthday present.

My few summer months as a recruit at Caterham were a period of conscious happiness. I had no responsibilities of any sort, almost every moment of my day being arranged for me. It was a gloriously hot summer, and I got more exercise in the open air than I think I had ever had before. My pay was so small—some of it was deducted as wife allowance, since I was technically married—that when I had bought my polishing materials and a few cigarettes I had enough left only for one or maybe two glasses of Guinness in the NAAFI. My new girl friend came down to see me on weekends, which we spent almost entirely in bed during the hours I was allowed out of barracks. The war seemed infinitely remote, a spectacle of vapor trails twisting against the azure sky. I had talked much about "the workers" but had never known any member of the proletariat with any intimacy. I did now, and discovered somewhat to my surprise that there was very little difference between the proletarians and the bourgeois, about the same proportion of likable and dislikable men, only the proles were much less educated and therefore generally more boring to talk to. Some were dishonest, some were lazy, some were downright stupid, others were pleasant, amusing, and agreeable. Being Irish, they lacked English snobbery and did not automatically dislike me for my educated accent, nor was I any richer than they. What difference there was between them and the middle class or the aristocracy was as nothing when compared to the resemblances and was certainly not worth a revolution. Conquest by a foreign power was another matter. At first I tried to discover why these peasants from Galway or Cavan, these gossoons from Dublin and Cork, Liverpool and London, had volunteered to fight for the traditional, national enemy. They could not understand my perplexity. There were two facts. One, the English were the traditional enemy (and they would have fights, particularly with the Coldstream recruits). Two, they had joined the Army. There was, in their minds, no contradiction between these two utterly different sets of facts. As for the Germans, they were simply "the enemy" and

might as well have been Frenchmen or Russians. Soldiers had to
have an enemy in wartime, and that was that. I found it all very
refreshing and educational. I was only disappointed by the fact
that their songs were vulgar hit-tunes and their singing was bad.
I suppose I had expected magnificent rebel ballads. Some forty
years later, and having spent a quarter of that time in Ireland, I
am still waiting to hear them.

I shall pass over the rest of my army career, which lasted until
1946, quite briefly. I loathed Sandhurst, which seemed to me to
combine all that was worst about Wellington and Oxford. Added
to which I had no money or credit. I drank as much as I could
afford. I was kept back at Sandhurst for one extra month, for
idleness: I spent most of it in the sanatorium, with flu, and was
commissioned into the Intelligence Corps. I was sent on a long
course, at a place called Matlock, and my report said that I was
not only idle but stupid. It added that I had the highest bar bill
of any officer who had ever attended the course. I was therefore
put in the infantry, and for a year marched about Northern
Ireland. After Pearl Harbor I applied for a transfer to the
American Army, which came through in late 1942. By then I
was back in intelligence work, and the Americans immediately
employed me on such work in London.

Now I was, by comparison with my friends and contemporaries, not only rich but had access, denied to Englishmen, to
liquor. I had acquired a new girl friend, Theodora, whom I sub-
sequently married, and we rented a pleasant little house in
Godfrey Street, Chelsea. I worked in Grosvenor Square and
would change when I came home, which was strictly illegal. We
would drink with our friends, Dylan Thomas, John Davenport,
Peter Rose Pulham, and others, in the local pubs and, when I
had drawn my liquor ration, at home. My work was interesting
and extremely secret. I was engaged on "ultra" work connected
with the planning of Operation Overlord. I can say with certainty—and I have had this confirmed recently by Theodora—
that no matter how much I drank I never betrayed or even
hinted at any knowledge I had acquired in my work. This may
have been because my life was split into two so completely sepa-
rate departments.

This lasted for over a year, until I went to France on General Bradley's tactical staff. For some months there was nothing to drink at all, though I do recall getting rather drunk in Chartres when given a day off. I think I did my work well, and certainly found it very interesting. I did not miss the drink, but on the other hand I never lost an opportunity to drink it when it was available.

Back in London for the last winter of the war, I resumed my double life, working at the War Office by day and drinking with friends in the Chelsea pubs by night. My work had become far less serious, and I was finally shipped over to a place near Washington for several months. The war was over now. I wanted out, and I wanted to write. I recall being acutely depressed at Camp Ritchie, but ascribed this to the fact that my wife was having an affair with another man in London.

This was the first and most acute experience of jealousy I have ever had. I returned to London, to my deserted flat, and would have shot the man if I could have found him. When at last I did, he was in a nightclub with my wife and I was unarmed. I quite exactly drank him under the table, and left him there, and took my wife home with me. A few weeks later we departed for America, demobilization, and Bermuda.

Such, then, in brief outline was my "prealcoholic symptomatic phase." It can, I suppose, just be fitted into the case of the young man, down from college, who gets married and starts to drink too much to please the boss in his office.

CHAPTER II

Alcohol

Alcohol, in the context of this book, is an addictive, sedative drug. In itself it is neither good nor bad. Indeed, as will be seen, it is usually benevolent, though this depends upon whether the drinker is a compulsive addict or not. (The nature of addiction will be discussed in the next chapter.) This bald statement is true of most addictive drugs, provided they are sensibly controlled. But, as will be readily seen even at this early stage, to write of the excessive consumption of alcohol is to move into a profoundly emotive field, in which such non-scientific words as "sense" and "control" abound.

There are many different sorts of alcohol, since its use is essential in many industrial processes. To distinguish these from the drinkable variety, various chemicals, such as naphtha, are added to pure alcohol, with the intention of making them too repulsive to drink or else of producing instant vomiting. These alcohols, in popular parlance, are usually lumped together generically as "methylated spirits," though methyl alcohol is only one of them. (Ether is the gaseous product of another chemical meld.) "Meths" is not in itself quite undrinkable. A really determined drunkard, deprived of his tipple, will drink meths, mixed with something pungent and even repellent. In England a mixture of meths and the cheapest red wine is known as "red biddy." At least one Soho pub occasionally frequented by this writer sold red biddy, almost openly, some forty years ago. It might be said that just as vintage brandies and ports are among the drinks of the very rich, so red biddy is the staple diet of Skid Row. Gross and repeated overindulgence in any alcoholic beverage may lead to an uncontrollable addiction or compulsion to drink, and the result is acceleration of the death process. There are, as will be shown, as many inhabitants of Skid Row living in luxury as on the Bowery.

Alcoholism is no more limited to one social class or sex of drinker than to any other; in this sense it is like any infectious or inherited malady. The simple essential, common to all alcoholic addicts and indeed to much else in life, is the bringing together of the addict and his drug. The most massive attempt to prevent this unfortunate encounter was the Eighteenth Amendment to the U. S. Constitution, which attempted to ban the sale of all alcoholic drinks to the entire population. (See Chapters XII and XIII). It was a complete failure; indeed it probably increased the alcoholic problem in the United States as more and more persons made their own (or bathtub) gin. Some found even this too laborious a process and made dry martinis with straight alcohol intended for commercial purposes but not yet turned into meths. In effect, just as the bottle of Old Grand-Dad, combined with venereal disease, did more to kill off the Red Indian than did the Winchester rifle, so the substitution of homemade red biddy did more to cause blindness and death, often by suicide, than legitimate alcohol had done. Diseases are quite uninterested in the wealth, beauty, or talent of those whom they attack. But fortunately only some six to seven per cent of drinkers are in effect potential victims of alcoholism. They, however, produce a further two per cent who will end up in Skid Row. And this is all the fault, chemically, of one manufactured product, alcohol.

Alcohol is no more and no less a drug than are marijuana (cannabis, grass: it has many nicknames) and cocaine. Like them it is *a sedative drug* not, as is often believed, a stimulant. It is easily available—never more so than during the Prohibition period in America (1919–33)—and is extremely easy to make. Since this book is not intended to make drinking easier, I shall not give the specifications of how to build a still. Suffice it to say that it is very simple. At one time a very high percentage of Irish farms had their own distilleries, which, if kept carefully, will produce a most pleasant and by no means "dangerous" drink (poteen), no more dangerous, that is, than whiskey. And its mere illegality added to the sadomasochistic pleasures and shame of drinking it.

Most country people have at least the vestiges of home distilling. In Normandy, homemade calvados (applejack) can be delicious. On many German farms *Schnaps* is distilled; in Northern Italy *grappa*. The Red Army carries unit distilleries on its strength, as other armies have bakeries. And one reason why these are everywhere illegal (save presumably in the Red Army) is that governments want the enormous taxes derived from liquor (and from cigarettes). To produce this vast revenue, taxes which should be crippling taxes are imposed, often up to 1000 per cent. A similar tax on the other now more or less acceptable drugs, such as cannabis, does not exist. The primary curse of governments, of virtually all governments, is their financial profligacy. But none has as yet dared impose a tax on teetotalers or nonsmokers. It would, it is true, be difficult to collect, save in certain, peculiar circumstances. When, for example, a Plymouth Brother is excused wartime military service, because his religion forbids all violence, the fact that the Brother's faith also forbids drinking and smoking surely should make him subject to a special tax? If a man cannot, for religious reasons, be a soldier, then if he may not fight for his country he should at least help pay for its defense. The reader must bear with my digressions. The important fact in this chapter is to establish the truth that alcohol is a sedative, not a stimulant.

Alcohol achieved notoriety as a stimulant precisely because it directly affects the entire nervous system selectively, making the higher centers of control less sensitive. This in due course enables the nerve centers to exact less restraint; that is to say, inhibitions, essential for any society, are partly numbed, and the drugged person will say and do things he or she would not otherwise permit him or herself. Hence a quite sincere belief that alcohol is a "liberating" drug. In a sense it is, but only in one sense, because it is concomitantly incapacitating. For with the abandonment of inhibition, part of a person's humanity is cast aside. A very simple proof of this is the slowness of speech and thought that accompanies the drunken state. Try recording a conversation, after half a dozen whiskeys have been lowered. Then play it back next morning. The resultant slowness, bad grammar, and foolish ideas are all that remain of last night's witty, even brilliant conversation. It is positively pitiful and can be infuriating. Because *alcohol is a sedative drug*, more so even than cannabis. And grass is not even taxed.

CHAPTER III

Addiction

The very slippery nature of the subject here under discussion, namely addiction to alcohol, is in no way more clearly identified than in the vagueness of many of the terms used. Not the least of these is addiction. And the trouble caused by such poverty of language (or by its plethora, too) is that each of us thinks he knows exactly what he is saying when he speaks of addiction. "Oscar Wilde said there's nothing easier than giving up cigarettes. He said that he's given them up himself at least thirty-five times."

Addiction is a pejorative word. It implies a compulsion to something that is in itself evil (tobacco gives you lung cancer is the gross oversimplification of the ill-defined cause-and-effect motif of cigarettes and cancer of the lung) or anti-social (pornography). However, an examination of at least one list of psychological compulsions unearths some peculiar ones: compulsion to work, for example, would seem to most of us a simple paradox, if the only results are exhaustion and unneeded gain. An addiction, in normal parlance, should inhibit or actually prevent work. Yet again, though, a closer look at this compulsive behavior does make sense. We all know, or know of, the businessman who can never escape from his desk. He brings his work home with him. His dinner guests are his workfellows. Holidays are a long frustration. An anecdote will describe the work addict.

A young member of a London banking family was sent to America to learn the American banking method. He was very keen, a real nine-to-fiver, once he even came in on a Saturday morning. On Monday a senior partner in the American banking house sent for him. The young man expected words of praise. Instead, what he got was: "If you can't do your work in five days, from about ten till about three, you have no business in a banking house at all."

In effect the young man's addiction to work was anti-social because it jeopardized the life-style of bankers generally.

And it is here that we are getting closer to the drink addict and further away from the cigarette addiction. Indeed even an anti-cigarette phobia can be very dangerous. A friend of mine is married to such a one. If the word "fiend" can frequently replace "addict" (i.e., a drug fiend, a fiend for unsweetened chocolate, etc.), then this hypochondriacal woman is an anti-cigarette fiend. By forbidding all smoking in her house, yes, even her husband's pipe, she has deprived him of almost all his friends, since he is too old to start frequenting bars or pubs. So there is a totally negative addiction—no one tries to make her smoke—which is as detrimental to one's family as are the "drink problems," with which we are here concerned, to many others.

A more fearful compulsion is gambling. Just as most people can and do drink in moderation, so a harmless game of bridge or even poker is no clue to a latent fanaticism, to an addiction. It is the man who plays cards or the horses way beyond his means who is an addict, though unlike alcohol this is a purely psychological and not also a physical addiction. And it is generally accepted that the absolute gambler does not play to win, but, unconsciously in all cases, desires to lose. He will not pocket his winnings but will continue at the baccarat table or the roulette wheel until he can turn his pockets inside out. It is in effect a variant of suicide in a society where money is the usual token of exchange and value. It is to be noted that many gamblers are also very heavy drinkers. As will be seen, the heavy drinker is in effect withdrawing from normal society. He has suicidal tendencies in that direction too. For alcoholism can be in itself a cause of death, though death comes to the person usually in a roundabout way, the motorcar being the instrument nearest to hand. (Thus almost always involving totally innocent people with no death wish whatsoever.) Cigarettes have been given a great fillip in the suicide stakes simply by the massive publicity given them lately as killers. Such deaths, however, will seldom involve others outside the immediate family, and I at least have never heard of anyone who smoked himself to death.

So let us now leave, at least temporarily, these poor people, the cigarette or cigar addict with his filthy morning taste in his mouth, the gambler who has just taken out the ultimate mortgage on his house, the work addict who has simply got his priorities all wrong, even the normal drug addict who lives in a twilight world of quasi-legal activity, the twilight made dimmer yet by his self-stupefaction, and let us concentrate on the addict to alcohol, the man whose sickness, aided by the internal combustion engine, has been named, by the World Health Organization as one of the three greatest causes of premature death that exist today after cancer and cardiac causes.

To sum up, then, in psychological terms addiction is an illogical compulsion to eat or drink or do. When the consumption or performance becomes psychologically harmful, in the first place to oneself, later to others, the fulfillment of the temporary craving ceases to be a mere bad habit and, where drugs are concerned, the harmful physical effect of their excessive use adds a real hazard to health and performance; then does the desire become, in the evil sense, a compulsive addiction. Drink is far and away the most common such. Taken in excess, it will destroy a marriage, almost any marriage: worse, it will destroy the family, which more than the individual is the essential unit of almost all societies; it will wreck a business or even a whole trade; it will emasculate military or naval units, even whole armies (Russia, 1905); it will lead to the premature death of the addict himself or herself, thus annihilating the family unit. It is not hard to see why the American anti-alcohol groups succeeded in the creation of Prohibition, in itself an admission that alcoholic addiction had become a national menace, nor why most religions have cursed it, in terms as excessive as the worst mouthings of the sick person. One confirmed addict will affect between five and ten other people, in his or her family, place of work, or site of enjoyment. It is alcohol, not the football itself, which often makes that popular sport the scene of mayhem, hatred, riots and, on occasion, death. Skid Row is not limited by class or income, intelligence or sex. And it is only with bad addictions that we are concerned. The so-called cures (there is no cure as yet known to medicine) can be almost as anti-social as the disease itself. For addiction to alcohol is a disease, and was identified as such as early as the first half of the last century. There will be more about the disease in later chapters.

Yet the drinking of alcohol, like any other widespread human practice, is not automatically the cause of misery. Medically it has been of the greatest possible value in many fields. Science has now, quite recently, produced more efficient and safer pain-killers and anesthetic drugs, and will undoubtedly produce more, but for centuries it was the only soporific or immediate sedative known to doctors. It was as valuable to the surgeon as it was to the general practitioner, perhaps more so in the days when surgeons were barbers. With most men, sufficient alcohol will lead to unconsciousness, "passing out." Such a condition was the best anesthetic a surgeon could hope for. But even then he had to be remarkably swift in his operation or amputation. Few people recovered from the shock, but there was more chance of the patient doing so if he was dead drunk. It was in effect the original wonder drug, but this again is straying from the subject of addiction. It is impossible to imagine a man or woman so addicted to alcohol that he will willingly lose his limbs in order to get, briefly, dead drunk. The psychological value of alcohol will be discussed later, and here, too, addiction will be examined in greater detail.

Meanwhile "addiction" as here used will have an evil meaning. It is a term that is used in medicine but has yet to be adequately defined. The addict of alcohol is often called an "alcoholic," a disagreeable adjectival noun of recent coinage. It will be used here as sparingly as possible, since it, too, has not been adequately defined. But here it will be used with reference, not to the heavy drinker only, but primarily to those who suffer from the equally ill-defined disease called alcoholism. We do not know why some people are compulsive addicts, others not. Indeed it has been said that everyone is, in some fields, an addict, whether the symptoms be excessive churchgoing, smoking, or even playing billiards. We shall leave Mozart to his billiards and listen to his symphonies. Even more obscure is why so many people choose alcohol as their sedative drug. The obvious answer is that it is so readily available. But since I can neither find nor create a copper-bottomed phrase to define either addiction, any addiction, and am therefore even less successful in pinning down "the alcoholic," the reader must accept these as shorthand words. For the truth is that in two vital ways *we do not know what an alcoholic addict is,* though we can usually recognize one quickly enough. But at least one point must be established immediately. *Alcoholism* is a disease and is no more "curable" than some cancers or diabetes. Neither of those is a sin, since neither has any deleterious effect on others, as does alcohol: there is thus no need for a Diabetics Anonymous, since there is no shame element. Indeed it may be that the shame or guilt or sin component is the most marked characteristic of alcoholism, and one with very few parallels in the twilight world of psychosomatic diseases. Gambling to excess is another most dangerous addiction. But we are no wiser as to why these death-wish addictions strike where they do.

This book is thus in large measure a quest for knowledge. By imparting to the general reader what I know (I am not a doctor, but even if I were I should still be stuck for absolute definitions) perhaps I shall encourage him or her to go much further than I can. Therefore, please do not read these pages as a textbook, for if you do you are likely to miss the point. To repeat, we do not know what causes any addiction or why so many addicts choose alcohol as the easiest way to play Russian roulette with their families, friends, employers, employees, and the unknown people in the other car. We do not know. Since almost everyone is affected by his or her or someone else's alcoholism, it is our plain duty, as thinking men with a social conscience, to try to find out. Once a cause has been established, it may be possible to find a cure. But it is very unlikely.

An alcoholic who was dying of cancer asked his doctor if there was any reason why he should not now drink as he wished. The doctor replied: "They may find a cure for cancer in your lifetime. They will certainly not find one for alcoholism."

CHAPTER IV

Alcoholic Addiction

Alcoholism is now generally recognized as a disease. It would seem to this writer, however, that alcoholism is a congeries of diseases, while addiction to alcohol is not automatically a disease at all.

Most people who drink—and this must include by far the greater part of humanity, as well as certain animals (elephants have a liking for fermented fruit)—drink regularly. That is to say, a man who likes his beer, maybe three or four pints in an evening, will drink these every day. If deprived of them he will miss his beer, but much as a "tea addict" will miss his afternoon cup or a "coffee addict" his breakfast drink. All three are addicted to his or her drink, its taste and its mild chemical effect (ethyl alcohol, caffeine) on his nervous system. Neither he nor those close to him will suffer from the effects of his addiction. This is as true of the woman who likes a cocktail or a whiskey and soda at six o'clock as of her grandmother who sipped a laudanum (an opiate) while dressing for dinner. In effect this mild form of addiction appears to be little more than a habit, to be almost natural. It is not. In historical terms the "discovery" of fermented drink, and later of distilling a stronger drink therefrom, is quite modern.

Let us take what we know of the history of alcohol.

Almost all races of man drink alcoholic substances, and have drunk them for a few thousand years. The exceptions are the original inhabitants of North and South America (here referred to for simplicity as Red Indians), though these did have mild fermented grain drinks; the Maoris of New Zealand; and the

Aboriginal inhabitants of Australia and its offshore islands. This
would indicate that alcohol as we know it was discovered in the
Eurasian land mass at a date later than the creation of the Ber-
ing Strait and the severance of the New World from the Old.
And other factors would indicate that it was discovered in what
is now China, though ancient Egypt also has a claim. The date
of this vital continental drift is still open to dispute, but it would
be reasonable to assume that alcohol was "invented" not much
earlier than some five thousand years ago and probably less.

We have many references to wine in our earliest Western literature, and some earlier ones in China. There are, however, only
two references to drunkenness in Homer, the Cyclops and Circe
incidents, which in view of the nature of the *Odyssey* is strange.
Also, one cannot help wondering what Achilles was doing all
those years that he sulked in his hut. The logical conclusion is
that wine came to the West at some point during the great mi-
grations caused by the creation of the Gobi desert. If we date the
Trojan War as having occurred some 1,400 to 1,200 years B.C., we
can be assured that wine was known then, but was probably a
rarity. There is, for example, no pictorial reference to wine,
though they may have had it, in the relics of Minos, which was
destroyed shortly after 1500 B.C. And the mythical legends—of
Bacchus or Dionysus—possibly came into existence somewhat
earlier. Originally wine must have been scarce, and its drinking
to excess—the Bacchanalia—an important quasi-religious ceremony. (But then what ceremony was not?) Let us then assume
that wine appeared as a rarity in Southeastern Europe sometime
before the Trojan War, and that the cultivation of the vine came
a little later. Spirits were unknown in the ancient world.

By the time of Christ wine was a normal drink, in particular at
ceremonies. There was already "good" and "poor" wine. (The
marriage feast at Cana.) It was also a common drink, used for
metaphor, as was bread for food. (The Last Supper.) Wine plays
little part in the Old Testament, save that its discovery, by Noah,
was a disreputable act and its excessive consumption by Lot
would indicate that it lay near the roots of the evil cities, Sodom
and Gomorrah. The Flood is also undated. But it is not hard to
equate it with the earthquake or volcanic eruption that de-

stroyed Cnossos. It would therefore seem fair to date the discovery of intoxicants at about 2000 B.C., or four thousand years ago. This is a twinkling of the eye in anthropological terms.

What we believe was later called chicken pox interfered with the Peloponnesian War, since this new disease met no built-in resistance and was therefore a plague comparable to the Black Death. German measles remains a plague to unborn babies, resistance apparently being built up only after birth. However, wine came originally in such small quantities that it scarcely assumed plague proportions. As its availability increased, so did the physical powers of resistance grow too. And virtually all who could afford it became wine addicts. They drank their wine watered. There must have been alcoholics in Greece and above all in Rome, but not in sufficient numbers to attract attention. The generally accepted figure today is that among drinkers some 6 to 7 per cent become alcoholics. The figures were probably the same in the ancient world. But had one of the emperors been an alcoholic, we should certainly have heard of it.

It is extremely difficult to find a medical definition of alcoholism. Indeed not everyone, or every doctor, accepts it as a disease even now, though the general informed consensus is that the 6 to 7 per cent of drinkers who fall into a certain category are sick. The definition, such as it is, is that when drink interferes repeatedly with a man's or woman's relationships with others, in the family, at work, even at play, then he or she is an alcoholic. It can also interfere in such mundane activities as driving a car, but again most drunken drivers are not medically definable as alcoholics, but many alcoholics are aware that they should never drive. From the scientific point of view this is all highly unsatisfactory in its vagueness and lack of precision.

There seem to be several ways of reaching the disease stage of alcoholism. One is the endogenous alcoholic. If he never drinks, then of course he cannot become an alcoholic. But he is one, all the same. I heard recently of a man of ninety who had never touched a drink. He had a mild heart attack and his daughter gave him a teaspoonful of brandy. His underlying predisposition declared itself at once and he died of drink three years later.

The second way is by birth (though this may be indistinguishable from the first). A Red Indian or a Maori has built up little or no resistance to strong drink, nor did it reach him gradually. For such people one drink is enough to produce drunkenness, followed rapidly by alcoholism and soon enough by death.

The third route to becoming an alcoholic, hard to distinguish from the second, is heredity. According to the Mendelian theory, heredity lasts five generations, or to a generation of ancestors numbering sixty-four. From any ancestor in this inverted pyramid, a child can inherit some or all of that person's characteristics. These five generations take us back some two and a half centuries. How many of us can identify his or her ancestors in 1750, let alone state that one of them was or was not an alcoholic? A few members of royal families, perhaps, or of the highest nobility. And it must be stressed that *heredity* passes *through* mother and father and is not inherited *from* them. And even if a total knowledge of one's ancestors c. 1750 were available, this still does not rule out alcoholism.

A fourth route, but one much overstressed, is environment. This can be in its turn divided in two forms which might be described as the subjective and the objective. The subjective will show the same man or woman in different circumstances. The most obvious, or at least the best documented, shows a man at home and at work, who gets on with his wife, likes his job and the pint he feels he has earned. Then war comes. All that is taken from him. Here is a quotation from Robert Graves's *Goodbye to All That* (concerning the First World War):

Officers had a less laborious but a more nervous time than the men. There were proportionately twice as many neurasthenic cases among officers as among men, though a man's average expectancy of trench service before getting killed or wounded was twice as long as an officer's. Officers between the ages of twenty-three and thirty-three could count on a longer useful life than those older or younger. I was too young. Men over forty, though not suffering from want of sleep so much as those under twenty, had less resistance to sudden alarms and shocks. The unfortunates were officers who had endured two years or more of continuous trench service. In many cases they

became dipsomaniacs. I knew three or four who had worked
up to the point of two bottles of whisky a day before being
lucky enough to get wounded or sent home in some other way.
A two-bottle company commander of one of our line battalions
is still alive who, in three shows running, got his company
needlessly destroyed because he was no longer capable of taking clear decisions.

In more mundane circumstances how often do we hear: "No
wonder he drinks with a wife like that" or "It's enough to drive
anyone to drink." Finally whole nations are driven to drink, so
miserable is their political condition. The Irish, under British
rule, were one example. The Poles are another. The French
phrase *"Saoul comme un Polonais"* was an expression used in
France to describe immigrant Polish coal miners. But the condition was created in Poland by German and Russian policemen.
And today, it seems, alcoholism in Russia may be a menace to
the state.

To be driven to drink by a nagging wife and to be an inherited
alcohol addict are not necessarily incompatible. Because here we
come to yet another type of alcoholic, who has neither inherited
the disease nor has it thrust upon him in the best behaviorist
fashion. A man or woman may drink, more and more heavily,
until he or she goes over the edge and becomes a fully fledged
alcoholic: of course there may be an alcoholic or more in his or
her Mendelian triangle: and there are always circumstances,
such as overwork or poverty or domestic troubles, that can be
advanced as an "excuse" for drinking so heavily and for so long.
The argument here is that just as there are great varieties of "the
alcoholic," so there are great, but converging, types of alcohol
addicts who will throw up the 6 to 7 per cent of incurable alcoholics.

For not only is alcoholism incurable, it is progressive. The person who knocks off drink in 1970 but goes back to it in 1980 has
not prolonged his health by ten years. On the contrary, *even
when he is not drinking* his susceptibility to drink increases, precisely as if he had never stopped. The old teetotaler of ninety
was as much an alcoholic as if he had been drinking for seventy-

five years. Had he remained sober for the remaining three years
of his life (which might have been five or even ten), he would
have died a natural death, as it was he died an alcoholic death.
We are mixed up in "ifs" and "buts." We cannot always be sure
where heredity ends and circumstance begins. Even the experts
can only guess, save in certain circumstances: the Red Indian's
reaction is usually biochemical. (See Appendix V.) But then is
it not all biochemical? What is nearer to certainty is to say that
the vast proportion of drinkers, even heavy drinkers, will not become victims of the disease called "alcoholism." Similarly, the only
way of arresting the disease is total abstinence, a quite unnecessarily disagreeable self-denial for most drinkers. But it remains
true that without alcohol there can obviously be no alcoholic addiction, without the addiction there can be no alcoholic disease.
With most Red Indians there is no need for the period of simple
addiction: he will jump straight into the disease, if he drinks at
all, and this is true of a proportion of non-Indians. This is particularly true of manic-depressives. And the manic-depressive is
very common indeed, though usually in too mild a form for con-
sideration here and his varying moods are more usually referred
to as "temperamental changes" or "feeling up and then feeling
down." The next chapter will deal in outline with depression and
drink, a vast subject and one touched on so far only by a handful
of experts.

CHAPTER V

Depression

There are two main forms of depression. The first and most usual is reactive depression, that is to say the depression created by circumstances ("No wonder he drinks, with . . .") and includes all forms of distress from a bad husband or wife to a bad government. It may also be a reaction against something which should, in theory, produce the very opposite of depression, such as winning the football pools in England or achieving sudden and unexpected good fortune anywhere, good fortune of such a nature as to result in a change of life-style, such as was the case with Marilyn Monroe. In my *Life of Dylan Thomas* I ascribed his insane drinking in America to the grinding misery of the income tax demands together with the sudden vision of good fortune achieved too late. One critic, Philip Toynbee, took me to task for not saying outright that Dylan was an alcoholic. Since I am still not sure what an alcoholic is, and since I stressed that Dylan Thomas drank to excess, I see less point in calling the poet "an alcoholic" than in giving his waist measurements, also caused by drink.

A medical biography of any famous man would be very interesting. An attempt to analyze the man would almost certainly be futile, as Freud himself admitted after his own attempt to analyze Leonardo da Vinci. Reactive depression, on the other hand, can often be traced to its roots, as with Byron's clubfoot or Toulouse-Lautrec's crippling smallness of physique. It is probable that both would have agreed: a sedative lessened the strain, and the easiest to hand was alcohol.

Endogenous depression, on the other hand, "grows from

within" (*Oxford English Dictionary*) and needs no external stimulus. It is inherent and therefore probably hereditary. (A doctor once made a very sweeping and certainly disputable generalization to me: all diseases that are not infectious or contagious are hereditary. Endogenous depression does not show itself at once, nor is it a permanent condition. At its gentlest it may be no more than a mild mood of "feeling a bit low today." As often as not a drink or two will dispel "the blues." On the other hand, if so treated the mood swing can become much more pronounced. And eventually alcohol, that most treacherous of friends and comforters, will take over. What was a mild mood swing can become a violent personality change, an almost Jekyll and Hyde syndrome. But if caught in time, endogenous depression will be too slow in its substitution of masks. At present much research is being carried out in a field where research is extraordinarily difficult, since so many words and terms are lacking precise definitions.

The Jekyll and Hyde parallel cannot be overstressed, for one of the most marked of alcoholic symptoms is the *personality change*. Perhaps the only widely quoted Latin tag these days is *in vino veritas*. This is quite untrue when the drinker is drunk. It is perhaps true when a few glasses of wine have dispelled certain superficial inhibitions and the drinker does not bother to conceal trivial matters. But if it were as simple as the cliché implies, how could any suspect of a crime conceal his guilt when given a bottle of whiskey? Lie detectors and lengthy interrogation would be unnecessary. If a secret is sufficiently important, it can usually be concealed, regardless of the amount of alcohol consumed.

Quite different is the *personality change*. We like to think of a merry, Falstaffian drunk. Such exist, but they are sadly rare. Far more common is the drinker who suddenly turns on the person he or she loves most, probably wife or husband, sometimes lover or even children. The affectionate husband becomes the embittered enemy who talks to hurt and who not infrequently is physically violent. This is not the "real" person but a travesty. Deprived of his inhibitions, he ceases to be a normal human being and becomes a beast. Nor do many women batter their babies when sober, though premenstrual and other tensions may be the cause. This does not mean that they *really* hate them, and that these emotions are let loose by drink. On the contrary, it means that at one end of the swing between mania and depression—the depression end—they have ceased to be their real selves.

The swing will then be reversed and the manic-depressive will end up in the manic state, a sort of euphoria, as difficult to live with as the state of utter depression, indeed in some ways more difficult, for the man or woman who has swung into euphoria will often think that this is the real self. But it is no more so than is the other. Psychiatrists regard both conditions as variants of the same sickness. However, elation is not "cured" by alcohol, while in the short run some aspects of depression are minimized. The term "depression" tends in itself to be misleading, since it is used in so many senses from economic to barometric depression. The simple English word "melancholia" would probably be more serviceable, as is hypomania for extreme elation. But then I am not here writing an improved medical dictionary. Suffice it to say that depression or melancholy, aided perhaps by an inherited tendency to addiction and often brought to the boiling point by reactive depression, is the most common cause of alcoholism. Wealth, good looks, brains, and talent cannot counteract this, though one or more of them may postpone and possibly diminish the virulence of alcoholism, while brains may help arrest it.

CHAPTER VI

Alcoholism v. the Heavy Drinker

In the jargon there is something called "social drinking," which, translated into English, means drinking for pleasure and not from compulsion. Many people, myself included, like to drink alone, not out of compulsion (though I am never far wrong when I know it is six o'clock, the sun is over the yardarm—there are scores more such expressions). But a man, and even more so a woman, who drinks secretly is almost certainly either an alcoholic or is associated with a wife or husband who has a phobia about the other's drinking. This is particularly true of certain religious sects which ban all drink as evil and call the "social drinker" a wicked man.

It has been reckoned, though obviously not confirmed, that among Mormons and Baptists, who ban all alcohol, no resistance is built up, so that one in three of lapsed Baptists and one in two of lapsed Mormons rapidly become alcoholics. However, there are other important factors involved, which will be dealt with later.

It seems to me that alcoholism is distinguishable from heavy drinking (let us at least dispose of the foolish and indeed meaningless word "social") only by its symptoms, some of which are as follows:

(a) Damage to, and ultimate destruction of, the family. As already stated, the basic human unit is not the individual, but the family group, which can be very large or limited to husband and wife or a homosexual equivalent.

(b) Repeated damage to work performance, ending in loss of job or collapse of business.

(c) Loss of friends who are not in the same condition.

(d) Physical deterioration.

(e) Poverty resulting from (b) and increased by the high cost of alcoholic drinks.

(f) Refusal to admit to an alcoholic condition.

The more obvious physical symptoms are:

a. Blackout. A certain type of alcoholic can drink all evening, appear moderately sober, and drive home. Next morning he will remember nothing, particularly where his car is. Occasionally those who were with him noticed nothing odd about his behavior.

b. Fights. The aggressive alcoholic is rare compared to the ordinary run of heavy drinkers. The fight in the pub will probably be a preliminary to the fight with the wife at home.

c. Vomiting.

d. Not eating. A good basis for the domestic fight, if the wife has prepared a meal for a husband who comes home drunk several hours late and then refuses to eat it.

e. Verbal violence. Boasting, usually but not always untruthfully.

The alcoholic may lack many of these symptoms; the heavy drinker may show several if not all of them. Where is the line to be drawn? The usual answer is that the alcoholic reveals, both repeatedly and *accelerando,* such symptoms as he does show. Further, that he will get drunk every night and a great many days, too. But still, such judgments as "he gets drunk before lunch" or even "he has several gins before breakfast" are not enough, though they are certainly indicative. Perhaps the only certain identification is that the heavy drinker who becomes ashamed of his drinking, or frightened, or both, is on the way to, if he has not already arrived at, an alcoholic condition.

The reader will now have understood how very unsatisfactory is the definition of "an alcoholic" and will realize the reasons for my antipathy to the word. There is no purpose in saying that this is all just a matter of semantics, that an alcoholic is an alcoholic and thereby the matter is opened and closed. But such rough and ready argumentation may well be true of other and indeed similar maladies. For example, a diabetic may be diagnosed according to strict medical procedure and the result can be positive or negative. A Wassermann test will show, beyond more dispute even than a diabetes test, whether or not the person is syphilitic. But an alcoholic has to be persuaded that he is an alcoholic. And this most people, even when their lives are being ruined by excessive drinking, ruined visibly and obviously not only to others but also to themselves, will have great difficulty in accepting. This reluctance is worth discussing here. For semantics, since they govern the truth or falsity of our communication with others, are of vast importance, and never more so than when we are discussing ourselves.

Most men, though rather fewer women, do not particularly object to being called—preferably behind their backs—a drunk, a drunkard, a lush, and the myriad synonyms. Some of them may resent being called a "problem drinker," since it too is a vague word. Whose problem? Well, frankly, your own and those who are close to you. All right, accepted. I must cut down. I know I can, since X months or years ago I gave up drinking altogether for Y months. Why did I start again? Why not? My friends all drank. Some had a drink problem not unlike my own. And did not Winston Churchill reply to his doctor who advised him to cut out the brandy: "It is a great mistake to tamper with the habits of a lifetime." I daresay I am not so good at my job as I used to be, but I'm still good enough. So was Churchill. To suggest that Churchill would have been a better man and a better Prime Minister if he had not drunk at all is grotesque. It is less grotesque to suggest that Hitler might have been less of a monster if he had.

The only proved method to free oneself of alcoholic addiction, once it reaches the stage of alcoholism, is to cut out all drink and forever. This is a drastic, often an impossible, decision for a person to take and to implement. Perhaps tomorrow? Or next week? Or when the symptoms outlined above become intolerable to the drinker, but not always then. Fear is seldom a definite argument. For most people the very admittance of fear conjures up numerous counteremotions. Who will admit he is a coward, frightened of debility or death at what seems long range? Another large scotch now cannot be fatal. Perhaps next month, next year . . . And even when writing these words, with honesty and I hope clarity, I am wondering whether a large scotch now . . . But there will be ample autobiography later in this book.

Shame is a far more potent force than fear, but it too can easily be counterproductive, can lead to secret drinking. And the next chapter will be devoted to this tragic subject.

CHAPTER VII

The Hidden Bottle

If there is some difficulty in distinguishing between the heavy drinker and the alcoholic, there is one quality which seems to be shared by all alcoholics (that is to say all victims of the disease alcoholism), and that is "secret" drinking. This is much more marked among women than among men.

For alcoholism is one of the few diseases that carry with them the moral condemnation of the victim, the venereal diseases being the most obvious. Nor is this moral condemnation utterly unjustified. A man or woman has got to drink before he or she can become diseased. No one is going to force drink down a person's throat. Only in very small pockets of society will a person be thought the worse for not drinking and, quite bluntly, for saying so. And nobody pretends to drink who does not, though I did once come across a curious phenomenon.

It was in 1945, in London, a time and a place where drink, particularly spirits, was very hard to come by. Dylan Thomas was staying with me and, as usual, we had gone out to the pub for a few beers. He, my wife, and I returned to my flat, entirely sober, to eat. I had acquired a bottle of Gordon's gin which had been drunk sometime before, but my wife had filled it with water, for some reason which now escapes me. Beside it stood a bottle of lime juice.

"Oh, good, gin and lime," said Dylan, rubbing his hands. And together we drank a bottle of lime juice and one of water. He became quite drunk, and next morning complained of a hangover. When I told him what had happened, he became incensed. "What a dirty trick!" he said.

From the psychological point of view the explanation of Dylan's hangover is both simple and obvious. So is the hidden bottle.

Alcohol is an acquired taste. For what reason will a young man acquire such an expensive taste? The answer is simple. Unless he moves in temperance circles, he will be surrounded by men slightly older than himself, virtually all of whom drink. By the mere fact of refusing drinks he will appear to himself childish and will fear that the others—who seldom in fact care—will regard him as priggish. No young man will wish to appear a child and a prig. Furthermore, since his companions obviously enjoy their drinks—as do his father and that generation—the taste is clearly worth the acquisition. If he has already inherited the qualities of an alcoholic, the acquisition will probably be easier once he has got over the disagreeable flavor of most drinks. (He might prefer a chocolate ice cream sundae, but that would surely attract attention to his youthfulness; besides, such babyish concoctions are seldom sold in bars, which are the places where men go.)

Very soon the addiction will have taken root. It may be and remain mild and harmless. But the ice is getting thin: the warning signs, such as the hangover, will disappear; to keep the blood-sugar level normal, more and more alcohol is needed; drunkenness becomes more common, with sooner or later all the more unpleasant symptoms.

It is at about this point that the drinker becomes frightened. He may well have seen some of his old friends become slaves to drink. He knows that he has said things, maybe to his wife, which come out of a bottle, not out of his own mind. It is, he realizes, time to take steps. He will cut down on his drinking, drastically. If he can succeed, well and good. His problem is solved.

But many do not succeed. They now start making promises, to their wives, to their bosses, even to themselves. They will never drink before six o'clock. For a time they keep this, but then what is one short drink at noon? Or two? Nobody will notice, particularly in a strange bar. And since the most ominous time is those "last drinks" at eleven or midnight, he will keep no spirits in the house. But suppose there was a crisis? He had not demeaned himself by hiding it. Yet she had made a scene when she noticed a bottle. It is therefore her fault that the next bottle is hidden, behind books, in the lavatory cistern, under the spare bed. And these bottles seem to go with remarkable speed. For by now the boy who wished to be a man is ceasing to be one, is becoming a clinical case of alcoholism. At last he realizes this, but it is too late. He will cut it out, entirely. After weeks of misery—days if he is weak-minded—he has forgotten the horrors and remembers only the warm glow. How delicious that first whiskey now tastes! How delicious the second! He is still technically a teetotaler, but the bottle is hidden again. Strange bartenders see a familiar type, unknown to them personally, who gulps down four or five doubles. His friends notice how his good humor has returned. Perhaps his wife does too, and may even congratulate him on his strength of mind. But sooner rather than later there comes the crash. Maybe she is clearing out the guest room. The empties have accumulated under the bed. If extremely tactful, she may try to say nothing.

But the game is up, and if he is a fundamentally honest man he will even be relieved that this is so. For all the lying and pretense are part, but only part, of the hellish web that alcoholism weaves around its victim.

CHAPTER VIII

Some Times, Some Places

We know little about drinking habits other than our own and perhaps those of our closest friends or lovers. To this minute basis of fact are added the fiction of the novelists but for the past two or three hundred years only, an occasional reference by the poet and the historian, and folk memories. Then there are the biographies of famous men and women, but they teach us little: who would dare compare the drinking habits of Maria Theresa and of Madame de Pompadour, let alone of Queen Elizabeth I with those of Catherine the Great?

What we do know a certain amount about are the drinking habits of various classes and groups of people at various times. Yet even here a lot remains speculation. With more precision we have religious teaching and dogmas. The Jewish faith is the parent religion of the Western world. It does not condemn wine as such. Indeed wine plays a minor part in some Jewish religious ceremonies, particularly the Passover. This has been inherited by the Christians; the Last Supper was the celebration of the Passover. But "wine-bibber" is not a polite denomination.

Muhammad forbade wine, all wine. As Norman Douglas once remarked, the prophet would have forbidden coffee and tea as well, had he known of them, since they too are pleasurable. And although many Muslims do not obey the law in respect to wine, a surprisingly large proportion do. Of course wine can miraculously turn to water when it touches the lips of an especially holy man, such as the Aga Khan, but such childish fabrications are not in general use.

The Christian religion has passed through a series of repeated reformations since the time of Luther and before, and almost all of these are marked by some form of teetotalism or at least by a condemnation of wine as a major sin. This is as true of the Roman Catholic brand of the faith as it is of the numerous Protestant sects, and the more extreme these are the more total is the condemnation of alcohol. On the one hand we have the strenuous efforts of Father Matthew in Ireland a hundred and forty years ago to induce the Irish to take an oath of teetotalism. He met with very considerable success, part of which endures. On the other hand, we have the extremist "low church" sects in Scotland as well as the Baptists and Mormons and some Christian Scientist and Quaker groups, no member of which is supposed to drink. And right across the whole Christian spectrum drunkenness is a sin, one of the seven mortal sins, the sin of gluttony. Here an important distinction must be made. Wine, or any distilled drink, is not in itself evil, save among such extremists as those referred to above: it is overindulgence, gluttony, which is the sin. And it is only fair to add that this sin is not taken particularly seriously, since so few drinkers imperil their souls. A man who habitually drinks too much will not necessarily regard himself as a bad Christian. The price he pays is more social than religious.

(I shall not deal with Hinduism or Confucianism or the other religio-philosophical creeds of the Orient, since I do not know enough about them.)

For many centuries, and in many parts of the world, the question "Can you drink the water?" should usually have been answered in the negative. Delphi, Bath, Tunbridge Wells, the various spas of Germany, France, Greece, and Italy were famous precisely because one could drink the water without being poisoned. This was true of many fast-flowing rivers, or at least their upper reaches: once they had passed through a major town, which deposited its raw sewage into them, or became tidal, the water grew foul and disease-ridden. Since most people did not live near a clean river, and since clean wells were not common, the answer was to drink something else. Speaking very roughly, in the northern climate this was beer—essentially fermented grain—and in the southern, vineyard countries it was fermented grape juice, or wine. The fermentation automatically killed the noxious germs in the liquid. And because of habit and example, this division in Europe between wine-drinking and beer-drinking areas corresponded roughly to the areas of the Roman Empire and to those beyond its limits. There were of course exceptions. Vines then grew in southern Britain, not in the north; Franconia had excellent vines. But in general the countries between the Rhine, the Alps, and the Mediterranean were inhabited by wine drinkers (the Rhineland and the Moselle Valley being the principal exceptions), those to the north by drinkers of beer, or even of mead, which is fermented honey. Savages from the extreme east apparently drank fermented mare's milk. Nobody drank spirits—except possibly some Chinese—since distilling did not reach Europe much before, if at all before, the fall of the Roman Empire. In a nutshell, therefore, during the long life of that empire the more civilized citizens drank wine, the less civilized beer, slaves and such water. It is much the same today.

The principle of distillation is extremely simple. Any fermented liquid contains, in liquid form, a small proportion of pure alcohol. The boiling point of alcohol is rather lower than that of water and most other common liquids. Therefore, if a fermented liquid is heated to, say, eighty-five degrees centigrade, the alcoholic content will become gaseous and can be separated from the rest. If this process is repeated, the brandy (a German word: *branntwein,* meaning "burned wine") will become increasingly pure alcohol. It will be colorless and, like vodka, almost tasteless, or flavored with, say, juniper as in gin. It can be colored, as with scotch, and flavored to taste. It can also be watered down. These trimmings apart, all spirits are the same, a burned, fermented drink with a considerably higher alcoholic content than the drink from which it was distilled.

Spirits, for drinking, can in fact be made from any fermented liquid. We have very early references from China, India and Tibet, where spirits—probably in China fermented rice wine—were made some two thousand years B.C. The Western ancient world knew how to distill—Aristotle distilled fresh water from salt—but strangely enough they do not seem to have used it for making spirits. The ancients did not often exploit their discoveries. But in their neglect of spirits from the Far East—and

trade was adequate—there may be another explanation. I have
drunk Chinese gin (I can think of no other word for it) only
once, but others who know China well have confirmed my opinion that it is the most disgusting thing ever to pass one's lips.
Perhaps the ancient world agreed unanimously. Another oddity
is that the Chinese never made wine, though they refer to grapes
for eating in the second century A.D.

The earliest reference to a distilled drink in the West is in the
work of the Welsh poet Taliesin, writing in the sixth century.
Grain spirit (in Ireland spelled whisky) was known long before
that in Ireland and Scotland. The story that it was introduced
into Ireland by St. Patrick should be treated with extreme caution. So should the legend that the Irish missionaries of the first
millennium brought a bottle of the hard stuff to help with their
conversions. But the name is definitely Celt, *usquebaugh,* or
"water of life," later translated, maybe by the Vikings, into the
Latinate *akavit.* Curiously enough it did not reach France until
the twelfth century, where like the wines it was named after the
area of its manufacture, Cognac, Armagnac, and so on, though
again *eau de vie* in general; and it was not manufactured on any
scale for another two hundred years. Virtually anything that is
fermentable can be distilled—rum from molasses and so on. It is
said that in the Second World War the Red Army fermented
and distilled grass.

But apart from the extreme Orient, whiskey was the first drink
to be distilled in any quantities, probably by the Irish and certainly by the Celtic-speaking Gaels. It seems to be the only invention that the Celtic-speaking peoples ever made: some would
say it was quite enough, both for pleasure and for pain.

Since this is not a technical or medical book about alcoholism,
I do not intend to describe in detail all forms of alcoholic poisoning. In any case, everyone knows that spirits are much stronger
than beer or wine. But since both contain alcohol, it is really
only a question of how much of each is drunk to produce the
same effect, and this has always been so. Seneca lived from 4 B.C.
to A.D. 65. His was a very trenchant if somewhat sour mind. (He
once remarked that the reason the slaves took to Christianity was
that they wished to have Sunday off.) His description of the

drinker, and his differentiation between the drunkard (alcoholic) and the man who gets drunk, not only is the earliest known to me, but cannot be improved upon, despite the invention of spirits. Marty Mann quotes it in her *Primer on Alcoholism,* and I give her translation here.

Posidonius maintains that the word 'drunken' is used two ways—in the one case of a man who is loaded with wine and has no control over himself; in the other of a man who is accustomed to get drunk, and is a slave to the habit . . . You will surely admit that there is a great difference between a man who is drunk, and a drunkard. He who is actually drunk may be in this state for the first time and may not have the habit, while the drunkard is often free from drunkenness.

This may seem a far cry, in time and space, from the Chinese and Irish and their drinking habits, but it is not quite so far as it seems. The Irish, both in Ireland and in America, where most of them live, have a firm reputation for drunkenness, made all the more remarkable in that the large population of Irish origin in South America is as sober as are most of the other inhabitants of that continent generally. This may be the heavy Red Indian influence, or some climatic factor, comparable to the Rhine-Alpine-Danube divide in Europe.

However, to return to Ireland: there is another oddity. As with the other Caucasian races, the percentage of alcoholics is believed to be the normal six per cent or so. But many Irishmen do not drink at all, either for religious reasons or because they have acquired a fear of drink from observing drunken parents or grandparents (Mendel's law may work in reverse, too). Therefore, among the Irish who do drink, drunkards seem to abound.

For some reasons which are obvious, and some which are not but will be dealt with, drunkards seek out one another's company. If they can find an excuse for doing this, so much the better. Great sporting events, perhaps particularly soccer in its various forms in the United Kingdom, are usually pretty boozy affairs, among the spectators of course. When the England-Ireland rugby international is held in Dublin, which it is every other year, great quantities of English rugger fans come to Ire-

land for the occasion. But is that the only attraction? How often
has one heard an English fan say, on his return: "Whew! How
those Irish can drink!" What he actually means is that he went to
Dublin, had a somewhat hazy view of the game, got plastered
for two days in the company of Irish drinkers, and returned to
his normal sobriety at home. But as will be seen, it is seldom
one's own fault if one gets drunk. Similarly, but far from making
self-excuse, Dylan Thomas once told me that his favorite city in
America was Chicago. "The best Skid Row in the States. Irishmen to a man." Since my own knowledge of Chicago is limited
to a couple of TV studios, where everyone was remarkably sober,
I cannot pass judgment on Dylan's appreciation, but I do know
that his belief that all American academics are drunk almost all
the time is not true. But then, a very high proportion of the
American academic population is of German origin, and this is
revealed in their prose and often in their thought processes
rather than in their revels. The hopelessly drunken Irish find
their natural habitat in Skid Row. The great German immigra-
tion of about the same date was not based to the same extent on
misery and famine, and there was no deportation. Therefore, the
Germans gravitated easily into the original Anglo-Saxon middle
class or into the farming community. Even as early as 1917 there
was virtually no pro-German lobby. They had become Americans in one generation.

CHAPTER IX

America, America!

It is with the American middle class that I intend here to deal, or, to be more exact, with some of its drinking habits, but there are two immediate and formidable obstacles. I must ask the reader to bear with me if I diverge as briefly as I can from the subject.

Class, in America, is a highly complex word, while the United States is an extremely large and diverse country—with Canada a continent as large and almost as complex as Europe. There is of course no aristocracy as such, though in certain small areas a few families will enjoy a position not dissimilar to that of the gentry in England or France. When they travel, however, they do not usually take their social status with them, and at home it can only be maintained if buttressed by wealth, since money, not birth, is the key to social superiority. This does not mean, in the usual oversimplification, that America is a plutocracy. What Americans, in general, respect is success, and since making money is the most immediately obvious form of success, a large earned income will very quickly place the man or woman high in the general esteem. (Another quick route to such esteem is massive publicity, particularly in the entertainment industry. Mediocre film stars are often more respected than dull industrialists, their political views being given much space, their marriages and divorces even more. Meanwhile the politicians, receiving usually more hostile than favorable comment, are not particularly high in the pecking order unless they are also celebrities. This is true of civil servants, generally regarded as parasites, and even of soldiers unless they hold the immense prestige of an Eisenhower or the film star qualities of a Patton. Undoubtedly Lindbergh is more famous than is Lemay.)

There is no such thing as an "American accent," though education is usually made self-evident by grammar. There are racial as well as local accents, and a Puerto Rican or a black man is often as quickly identified by his speech as by his pigmentation. The bad phraseology of the poor white will also preclude him from "society," though he will be accepted if he makes money. Immense and largely successful efforts have been made in the last generation to overcome racial prejudices. It would not be surprising, nowadays, to find black people, a few black people, at a Boston dinner party, only rather more surprising to find them in Charleston. But they will be lawyers or doctors, not the inhabitants of places like Harlem. This is only logical. And since white Americans are in a huge majority, it would be foolish to expect much more than a very small percentage of the guests to be black even if all racial prejudice were totally eliminated.

Therefore, what the majority of Americans are in fact aiming at is a measure of wealth and respectability. The average American is an almost impossible paradox, but what makes him average is that he will belong to, or aspire to, what in other countries is called "the middle class." The proletariat in America will seldom admit that it is such, and social mobility therefore replaces social revolution. The result has been that "the American" is a definite and recognizable type of man, in many ways more so than the Frenchman or the Italian. With vast exceptions the American will wish to be like other Americans (the melting pot) and he has in large measure succeeded. One important form of emulation is in his eating and drinking habits. On the whole, American eating habits have produced a healthy, wholesome diet, though the monotony of the food will sometimes depress foreigners. Drinking is what concerns us here, not Skid Row or fanatical teetotalism, or the film or sports stars or multimillionaires, but the way of drinking of the "average" American man and woman as defined in this paragraph. Let us take the small businessman, married and with two teen-age children, living in a small suburban house, with an income rather in excess of ten thousand dollars per annum. His name is not Babbitt, but it might have been his maternal grandfather's. Let it be his, in respectful memory of Sinclair Lewis, who knew him well, pitied him, and took to the drink instead.

Young Babbitt, not so young at forty-two, had little interest in his family background. He knew that his grandfather had made a certain amount of money and had heard that his father had spent most of it, apparently on bootleg gin, and died at fifty. His widow had never allowed her son to forget the evils of drinking, but he had never taken this very seriously, drinking moderately at college and quite heavily with the boys in Korea. Home with his bride and soon the children, he had had no drinking problem. His job in the offices of the paper factory satisfied him, and the pay would improve. He had only once been unfaithful to his wife (when on a business trip), and he blamed this on the Bourbon his hosts had given him. He was ashamed and frightened, too, lest he had contracted a disease. But he had not, and quite quickly the shame had faded, the memory vanished. He assumed, and correctly, that his wife had never been unfaithful to him, and incorrectly that his sixteen-year-old daughter was a virgin.

There would be small purpose in describing Chuck Babbitt's day, from the orange juice, thermos cup of coffee, and the dish of cracklipops, through the pile of uninteresting papers to be signed, marked "passed to," on one occasion "not for me". Lunch was a glass of milk and a bacon and peanut butter sandwich. Occasionally Chuck would slip out with Bob Little, who worked in the next office, and they would have a beer together. Bob in fact did this most days, perhaps having something even stronger, but today in particular Chuck was being extra careful. At five-thirty Bob came into the room without knocking, and stood with his hand on the door.

"One for the road, Chuck?"

"No, thanks. Anyhow I haven't quite finished."

Bob hesitated, "Going to the Dolmetches' cocktail party?"

"I guess so."

Chuck reached for a paper from his in-tray. He wondered why Bob was so hesitant.

"There's a cousin of my wife's, Charlie Lomas, hardly know him. Says he knew you in Korea. Same name, anyhow."

Chuck looked up with some surprise, "Whirlybird Charlie? Course I know him. He in town?"

Bob nodded, "Sure you won't have that drink?"

"No, thanks. There'll be plenty at the Dolmetches'."

"I guess so. You know, I dread these parties."

Chuck saw that his in-tray was empty, "The women like them. Maybe I will have that drink."

"Attaboy. Let's go."

The bar was almost empty and also almost pitch dark. Chuck put his glass down, forcefully, "Must go, Bob. It'll be good to see old Whirlybird again."

"Sure you won't? Yes, he wants to see you, too. Quite a guy."

"See you at the Dolmetches'."

He turned the key in his front door and immediately heard his daughter's sniffling from the kitchen. The unattractive sound redoubled as his wife opened the kitchen door.

"Chuck, you're late. We'll be late for the Dolmetch party."

"She said six. That means anytime after six. What's the matter with Cindy this time?"

"Come on in here." She led him into the living room.

"Chuck, she thinks she's pregnant again."

"What do you mean, again? She's never been pregnant."

"She's three weeks late."

"I don't understand. Haven't you told her the facts of life? That she won't get pregnant necking?"

"Three weeks, Chuck."

"Then take her to Doc Hanlon again. How can you expect me to understand these things?"

"I thought you'd be a little more sympathetic."

"Sympathetic? Sympathetic about what? I'm not a woman and I'm not a gynecologist, and I thought everybody knows how to make babies and they take their pills."

Mrs. Babbitt was dabbing at her eyes, "It's easy for you."

That second whiskey with Bob Little was beginning to have an effect.

"What's easy for me? Living in a house full of whining women? I have to go change."

The Dolmetch cocktail party, so like the normal run of these about-once-a-week events, can best be recounted in quasi-statistical terms. Mr. and Mrs. Babbitt arrived at six twenty-five, the seventh and eighth of twenty-five guests. The basic drinks were dry martinis—passed on a silver tray by Mr. Dolmetch's son Lance—or scotch and soda, available at a small bar in a corner of the living room. Some ten people might have sat: none did.

Chuck and his wife, who was called Lousa (not, as she constantly pointed out, Louisa: nobody ever asked her why), had hardly spoken during the drive, and as soon as he decently could he left her to make his way across to the scotch, where Bob Little already was, with his cousin-in-law, an Air Force captain known as Whirlybird, since he had once been a helicopter pilot but for many years now a desk officer.

At six thirty-five Mr. and Mrs. Carter arrived. He was Bob Little's and Chuck Babbitt's boss, so both their wives were especially attentive. Mrs. Carter made her presence felt by asking for a dry sherry instead of a martini, and Mr. Carter raised his right hand in a gesture of refusal, "Not for me. Never touch it. Just a glass of fizzy water—you know, Schweppes, something like that."

Mrs. Dolmetch tried to dissuade him from this slightly unusual drink, offering several sweet alternatives, such as Coca-Cola or Seven-Up, but Mr. Carter was adamant. So Lance was sent away.

At six forty-two Mr. Carter, now equipped with his fizz water, leaned forward and said to Mrs. Little in confidential tones: "Is Bob all right?"

She smiled bravely, "Fine. He's over there." She pointed toward the bar. Whirlybird had just finished an anecdote. The three men had thrown back their heads in a great burst of laughter.

Bob asked Lance: "Do we help ourselves?"

"Sure."

Mr. Carter's eyes returned from the laughing men. He said to Mrs. Little: "I've been a little worried about Bob lately."

Mrs. Babbitt was leaning forward so as not to miss a word.

"Oh, Bob's fine, Mr. Carter."

The conversation around them might have been that of a statisticians' congress, the price of vegetables, the value of property, the cost of a new road, the rainfall in inches. Mr. Carter said: "I think he needs more exercise. You should see he gets more fresh air."

"Oh, I don't know, Mr. Carter. He plays golf."

"Mostly on the nineteenth green, if you'll pardon the expression," then turning in a stately fashion to face Mrs. Babbitt: "How would you feel, Mrs. Babbitt, if I were to recommend Charles for a promotion? No, not so fast!" He held up his hand. "It would involve a move. But your boy's in college already, isn't he? And pretty girls are everywhere."

"Why, Mr. Carter!" Her voice was drowned by another and louder burst of laughter from the bar. Mrs. Babbitt had to repeat: "Why, Mr. Carter. This is so sudden. Chuck said nothing—"

"In my household Mrs. Carter always makes the decisions. I believe it's the same in all sensible households."

He gave a small, stately bow, followed by a small burp.

At seven five the alcoholic level in Bob Little's bloodstream passed that permitted by highway regulations. Whirlybird was a little ahead of him, Chuck a little behind. The room was getting blue with smoke.

Whirlybird said: "We can't just stand here. Lunch tomorrow? No, it's Saturday. You can play golf anytime, Bob. My hotel, at one o' clock. Okay? No women."

Chuck said: "Yes. Now excuse me."

He had seen Dr. Hanlon, standing near the door, refusing a cigarette. Charles knew that he was saying that even ten minutes more of life was worth more than a smoke.

"Hello, Doc."

"Hi, Charles."

"Doc, I've got a problem. Can we move over here?"

They edged into a corner. Dr. Hanlon said: "I wish I could go somewhere sometime where nobody had a problem. I'm told it's the same with priests. Well, Chuck?"

"It's Cindy. Thinks she's pregnant."

The doctor took a cocktail from the passing tray. Chuck nodded at his scotch and soda.

"Another, Mr. Babbitt?"

"Yes, please, Lance."

"Cindy?" said the doctor. "I wouldn't have thought she was the type."

"Nor would I. In fact I don't believe it."

"And you'd like me to take a look at her?"

"That's right. I know how busy you are."

"I'll be away all next week. I don't like working Saturday mornings, after I've finished at the hospital. But bring her over at a quarter past twelve."

"Gee, that's good of you, Doc. I'm sure it's nothing. But Lousa is worried."

"Of course. How old is she?"

"Just sixteen. Listen, I'll get Lousa to bring her over."

"Yes, that might be better. Good martinis Dolmetch makes."

"I prefer this."

"You want to watch out with that stuff. They're doing something with the whiskey these days."

"They've got real competition now that cannabis is legal in half the states."

"Keep off that, Chuck."

"Oh, I will."

It was seven fifteen and his blood alcohol level now made it illegal for him to drive.

The cocktail party lasted until nine. Chuck drove home, slowly and carefully. Cindy was out. He and his wife had the worst fight of their married life. She even threatened divorce. Neither of them took this seriously.

Six weeks later Mr. Carter more or less ordered Bob Little to accompany him to a meeting of Alcoholics Anonymous. By then Cindy knew she was not pregnant, and they all lived happily ever after.

CHAPTER X

Ye Olde Englishe Pubbe

"Drunk as a lord." It is a curious expression, and one that is still current usage in England and America, though not, I think, anywhere else. It is a phrase that is not easy to dissect in this period of social change in England. The drunken lord is not the impoverished peer trying and failing to farm the hundred-odd acres that are all that successive death duties have left of a once vast estate, while he lives with his lady in what had been one of fifty cottages and observes the busloads of summer trippers enjoying the large house-turned-museum. Nor is he an intoxicated Labour Party or Conservative nominee to the House of Lords, living on his sinecure salaries as a director of companies, and often attending the House merely for the sake of a retainer that will buy him a couple of bottles of scotch. No, we must go back further, to the archetype.

He is probably best found in the mid-eighteenth century. He lives in the large house, with a mass of servants. His farms prosper, his tenants pay their rent, the Anglican clergyman is a man of his choice, and the village pub is named after his arms. The London coach passes through the village once a week, but his lordship has his own carriage. He hunts, shoots, and fishes by day. By night he drinks and not infrequently gambles. Save when he loses heavily at cards, he is a rich man. He is moderately interested in politics, and regards it as his duty to go to his London house, even out of season, and vote on important issues in the House of Lords. He is extremely patriotic and antidemocratic. He is quite well educated, has toured Europe and returned convinced that popery is dangerous mumbo-jumbo and that God inspires the views of the English nobility.

His evening meal, held at about dusk in the wintertime (after the shooting) and later in the summer, is a gargantuan repast washed down with several wines. The ladies then leave the gentlemen to their port and Madeira. Those he may drink in enormous quantities. Chairs of the period exist with rockers instead of legs, so that the lord and his guests cannot fall out of them or trip them. In middle age his eating and drinking habits are likely to produce gout and liver complaints. He may drink brandy, over cards after dinner, whiskey probably seldom, and gin not at all. By the time our prototype is helped up his handsome staircase to bed, he is indeed as drunk as a lord.

There were of course many English noblemen whose home life was very different, just as there are many Americans who have never attended a Dolmetch-type cocktail party. Yet there is usually a reason for a popular phrase. Lineaments of Charles James Fox are detectable in such otherwise totally diverse political characters as Rochester, Palmerston, Asquith, Winston Churchill.

As is known, the English love a lord and they seem to like their lords to get drunk. This may be a simple form of identification. The peasants would also like to get drunk, but can seldom afford to do so. The lord of the manor, of their manor, can and does—he is indeed "to the manor born." Hence the expression, which is not one of acrimony or jealousy as a similar phrase (none exists) might be in France or Germany or Italy.

So let us glance at the drinking habits of the countrymen who were not lords, in the period of which we have been talking, and see how these have developed in the two centuries that have since passed.

With the exception of London, the cathedral cities, and a few ports, England was a rural community upon which the first industrial revolution had only just begun to break. And as the next chapter will show, London was very different. The usual drinking place, in country villages, was the village pub.

Many of the million or two of American soldiers who passed through Britain during the Second World War returned home filled with enthusiasm for "the English pub," and indeed the word has caught on in America to some extent. Therefore let us examine the English pub, both rural and urban.

In almost every field of activity, the English have always been intensely class-conscious. So are most nations, but there is a rigidity about English class distinctions that is perhaps unique. (Social mobility is irrelevant. Once high status is achieved the newly arrived Englishman is perhaps even more starchy than his new peers.) The lord of the manor did not get drunk in the pub named after his arms. It is most unlikely that he would do so today. But it did not occur to the peasant that he should be allowed to drink port at his lordship's table. In *Far from the Madding Crowd,* Thomas Hardy describes a feast held at the manor house, to which all the villagers were invited, a little less than a century ago. The great emotional strength of the chapter is the rarity of the occasion—once a year—and the element of bewilderment it engendered. But then the owner of the manor was a remarkable woman, Bathsheba Everdene, who herself came of more humble stock and was not to the manor born. Hardy saw through and disliked the essential phoniness of English class distinctions: most Englishmen, and of all classes, did not, even when they became urbanized. It may be changing now, and class distinction may be becoming class war, but this is one hundred years later than Karl Marx had anticipated, and nearly seventy years since Lloyd George (a Welshman, be it noted) set about the ruination by fiscal means of the aristocracy.

The villagers were very poor. They became poorer throughout the eighteenth century, partly owing to the enclosures by the landlords of what had been common land and partly owing to the rapid decrease in the infant mortality rate, with consequent overcrowding. For the peasantry overcrowding meant not only pressure on the space in their cottages, but also on the ground that was theirs, for their own food. There were an increasing number of "improving" landlords, but perhaps the rosiest picture of village life at the time is still Gray's *Elegy,* the dreariest Goldsmith's *Deserted Village.* And in large numbers the villagers did desert their overcrowded villages, often for New England, there to attempt to rebuild the prototype. When the GI of 1942–46 carried home with him a nostalgia for the English pub, he had in effect been moved by a glimpse of an important part of his own country's prehistory.

Shopping was a rarity, for the shops were in a nearby country town, and the villagers bought little. How could they? Money was also a rarity. The center of the village was, hierarchically, his lordship's manor; in religious terms the Anglican Church, which had little other than spiritual comfort to offer; socially the alehouse or pub. It was there that the pennies were spent.

A few of these archetypal village pubs still exist. The essence is the landlord. He must be first of all friendly and secondly honest (with his local customers he has little choice in this, though I did hear of a publican in Essex who persuaded the GIs that there were ten pennies in a shilling, and gave change accordingly). The pub should be clean, with a warm fire on winter evenings—the villagers could sometimes afford only an occasional fire for cooking—and games were provided, dice, darts, dominoes, shove-ha'penny, cards, even sometimes skittles. The amount of conversation available to the villagers was limited, and these games of luck or manual skill were a pleasant way of passing the time. The drink was beer from the local brewery, which often owned the pub. It was cheap, and it had to be, for the villagers had very few pennies. There was therefore very little drunkenness. Only for the great private festivals, weddings, christenings, funerals, and the public ones, Christmas and Easter, would they dig into their tiny capital, and sometimes the lord of the manor would help out. It is the custom of the British and the Irish to celebrate Christmas and Easter by getting drunk, which may strike some people as odd. This may be one reason why the New England tavern had little in common with the Old England pub.

When the coaches began to traverse England, they would seldom stop in the village. The inn came into existence in the towns —it already existed in the larger ones—and immediately class distinction arose. The inn was the best, or largest, pub in the small town. Meals, beds, stabling were provided, and perhaps one bar set aside for the local beer drinkers. It was from the inn, not the village pub, that the rolling English drunkard may or may not have made the rolling English road: despite G. K. Chesterton's jolly couplet, it was more likely contours and territorial boundaries. In rural, preindustrial England the drunkard seems to have been a noticeably strange figure, and the reason for this was as much economic as moral. The workingman who suddenly had silver in his pocket seems to have spent it on drink. The "drunken sailor" is the classic example. He has been paid off, and his pay goes on drink and women. He would hardly be seen in the village pub, any more than the lord of the manor, who had silver in his pocket every night.

The massive emigration to the new cities, horrible slums in our eyes but often luxurious to those who came from the decaying, overpopulated rural slums, brought a number of marked changes, perhaps the principal one being that the workingman and woman and child received his miserable pay in cash. And just as in his village he had spent virtually all his pennies on beer, so now he spent far too much of his family's earnings on beer and later on the newly imported spirits. He often still does, particularly on payday.

Hogarth preserved the antithesis in his "Beer Street" and "Gin Lane." The evils of Gin Lane were transported across the country in the nineteenth century by the great gangs of itinerant laborers, largely Irishmen driven from their own country by famine, who descended for brief periods on the villages through which the canals, railways, and then the new roads were being built. Increasingly heavy excise on spirits, however, drove the average workingman back to his beer. And in the working class districts of the cities, including London, a distinct echo of the village pub was to be found in "the local." It was perhaps this that the American soldiers saw and appreciated.

By the Second World War the English class structure had of course changed drastically, but class distinctions were at least as marked as they had been in the eighteenth century. Though there were still rich and poor, and a large middle class, its members aspired rather less than their American equivalent to great wealth, while the working class even less to a middle class status. Some areas of London, in particular the East End, were almost homogeneously working class, but in most boroughs classes were mixed. In the pubs this was made evident by different types of bars, charging different prices, from the saloon to the public. The rich seldom went to pubs, save perhaps to buy a bottle to take home, their women virtually never, while the

men had their clubs. The saloon bar would be for the shop-
keeper class and in some areas students, very few of them
women. Here spirits would be drunk as well as beer. The public
bar was also known as the four ale bar. Its name is indicative. As
well as members of the working class, again with very few
women, men who wanted as much drink as they had money
would frequent this bar. It was usually here that pub fights
broke out (they were rare) and that the real drunkards were to
be found if the landlord did not have them ejected.

All this changed with the Blitz of 1940–41. After a bad night
people of all sorts went to their local for a drink and, perhaps
more important, to exchange the local news. The presence of
men in uniform did not alter this, for they were usually at home
on leave. The Blitz, for a while, did a great deal to destroy class
distinction in London and the other bombed cities, reinforcing
the solidarity that goes with war.

Once the Blitz was over, this habit of drinking in the local by
all classes continued and was strengthened by the extreme
difficulty, amounting at last to near impossibility, of buying a
bottle of anything to drink at home, while for the men, traveling
to and from their West End clubs in the blackout was not pleasurable. Women, of all classes, by now frequented the pubs quite
unashamedly.

Such were the pubs the GIs saw, quite unlike anything they
knew at home. And their judgment was correct. Despite the rep-
etitious, "Sorry, no spirits" and the need sometimes even to bring
one's own glass, despite the crowding and the tendency to
drunkenness where often the man or woman would have gotten
drunk at home, they were warm and pleasant refuges. Perhaps
even something atavistic had come back from the old village
pub. This mingling of the classes was surely a sign of health and
strength.

Unfortunately the near classlessness of 1945 did not long survive. In some ways class spread, the wives of skilled workers regarding themselves as socially superior to those of men only
semi-skilled. And the Welfare State introduced a creeping tone-
lessness. In the pubs this was emphasized by a vast amalgama-

tion of their owners, the breweries, which led to a somewhat un-expected form of standardization.

For some time spirits remained hard to get, and the rich there-fore continued to frequent the pubs. Indeed this became and has remained a habit among certain elements of that class, particu-larly on Sunday morning. Equality of the sexes, too, prevailed. And this was, for the brewers, a lucrative trade which they were anxious to preserve and if possible enlarge, while the quality of the mass-produced beer declined.

Saloon bars had been slightly more comfortable than public bars, but had retained the basic pub image, oaken tables and benches, stools, many mirrors advertising whiskeys, in gilt, per-haps a bar billiard table, plank floors, in general a mixture of wood and glass. Now, with redecoration, most of this went. In-stead, a sort of mock drawing-room was created, with uphol-stered furniture, fewer tables closer together, wall to wall car-peting, fashionable prints instead of mirrors, sometimes a snack bar serving exotic dainties (some old pubs had provided bread and cheese and pickled onions at lunchtime). In some pubs the public bar was abolished altogether, and the whole of the street level floor became not unlike Mrs. Dolmetch's living room, with Muzak added. Where the public bar remained it, too, was tarted up and with a television set. Does anybody play shove-ha'penny anymore, now that the halfpenny has ceased to exist? And all this was certainly not the fault of the American servicemen. It is by some strange form of osmosis that dry martinis are often now-adays served instead of bitter beer in The Red Lion.

CHAPTER XI

Liquor and the Law

Since alcohol is a sedative that stills inhibitions, the man who has drunk a good deal ceases to be his "normal" self, at least in the eyes of others. In the company of his friends he will probably talk, and above all laugh, more loudly. His critical faculties become less active. Jokes are funnier; serious conversation seems to be more profound. He may well be indiscreet, and to his friends amusingly so. He, and she, will be more openly amorous.

> Candy
> Is dandy
> But liquor
> Is quicker.

This sort of drinking most people regard as pleasurable, though to the man or woman who is entirely sober a live Falstaff may seem moderately tedious, as Shakespeare's did later when Henry became king. But to the majority, particularly of young people plagued by shyness, drink is a passport to gaiety, sometimes to wisdom if he or she is in the company of older, wiser people, for distinctions of age and knowledge become blurred and forgotten. In Puccini's *La Bohème* perhaps the song *viva la compagnia!* gives the finest musical rendition of such joyous occasions, when wine maketh glad the heart of man. A football team, already linked by the companionship of the game, will become yet friendlier over the beer. So will the farm laborers as they play their games of darts in the English country pub.

There is another pleasant way of drinking which is also, but incorrectly, described as "social drinking." A man or woman after a tiring day of labor, whether physical or mental, will appreciate a drink alone as much as in company. A "pick-me-up" will wash away the worries, anxieties, even the exhaustion of work. Then a good meal, a comfortable chair by the fire on a cold night or in a garden on a summer's evening, a good book, a whiskey and soda, maybe a cigar, all these can produce a very real sensation of well-being.

Drink has many other pleasures to offer, not least that of taste, from the great wines to a good beer or a well-mixed dry martini. It has been said that these tastes are "acquired," as if that were a pejorative, but then so is a taste for oysters or caviar, even for Cézanne or Chaucer.

It is hardly surprising that almost all mankind, everywhere and at all times, has praised Bacchus. If a man or woman gets drunk, in Seneca's sense, the only cost is probably a slight headache next morning.

Not all drinkers react in this way, or for very long. The "personality change" will also release the drinker from useful and easily acceptable inhibitions, sometimes immediately, more often after a shorter or longer period of heavy drinking. This can produce the well-known "drunken bore," repetitive, verbose, sometimes maudlin and given to self-pity, that most useless of all emotions. It can also produce the "fighting drunk," the instigator of pub brawls and later of domestic fights. He will become idle, spending his time drinking rather than working, and will not infrequently take up a life of petty crime to get the money he does not earn. And it is now that the law steps in, as Seneca's drunk becomes Seneca's drunkard. And his haunts, which will now be usually urban, are very far from the idealized English country pub described in the previous chapter.

The drunkard has been condemned or labeled, at various times, as a sinner, a criminal, a lunatic, and, quite recently, as the sufferer from a specific disease called alcoholism. On occasion he is in fact none of these, on occasion all four, and the emphasis is often determined less by his behavior than by the mores of the society in which he lives. In Puritan America, for instance, sin was uppermost, and this spread across the States throughout the nineteenth century. It is still so considered by many, including a high proportion of the clergy of all faiths. In this century, however, the growing American infatuation with science has thrust the disease syndrome to the fore, and this was given a great boost by the importation of psychiatry and psychoanalysis into the United States some fifty years ago. The behaviorists, on the other hand, who attempt to make environmental conditions the cause of every evil, have naturally applied their dogma to the drunkard, sometimes justly so. Certainly there is more obvious, obnoxious, even dangerous drinking in the streets of slums and shanty-towns than in more prosperous residential areas. And this in turn brings in heredity, to which the environmentalists are in general opposed on ideological grounds, because if weaknesses can be inherited, so presumably can strengths, if vices then virtues.

Finally the blame can be taken off the drunkard almost altogether and ascribed to the drink, "demon rum," and above all to the bars and saloons in which it is most conspicuously consumed. In America the underlying emotive force that inspired the many temperance movements of the last hundred fifty years was the wish to stamp out sin, while the political and hence legal motive was a dislike of the saloons, many of which became politicized. In England, on the other hand, the law stepped in at a very early stage and largely to protect property, particularly in London. Dean Swift was probably the first prominent man to express charity for the drunkard, as for the mentally ill in general, and, what is more, to put his charity into practice.

In the Middle Ages the English enjoyed among their neighbors a reputation for heavy drinking. But what those neighbors saw were English soldiers. A man who would join a medieval army was likely to be "brutal and licentious" or, if press-ganged, could easily become so. When the wars were over, both the French wars and the Wars of the Roses, a great many soldiers were without employment and were known collectively as "sturdy beggars." These unemployed men gravitated to London, and in the late fifteenth century crime and disorder were being associated with public houses there. In 1551 alehouses were first licensed, being described as the resort of idle and disorderly characters. Throughout the Tudor century England was passing through a long period of economic depression, as the Spaniards, the French, and the Hansa ports gained predominance in European trade. The unemployed also gravitated to London and joined the sturdy beggars in the alehouses, where the sale of wine, being stronger than beer, was immediately forbidden, in 1552.

Since that date there has been such a mass of English, later British, legislation that it can only be touched on here. In 1625 a law was passed imposing fines on drunkards and, significantly, on publicans who sold drink to drunkards. It would seem probable that Cromwell's New Model Army and the largely Calvinist army of the Scots were far less drunken than the Cavaliers. Their puritan virtues won them little popularity with the people as a whole, and with the Restoration a general relaxation of publicly enforced morality was inevitable.

Then, in 1690, spirits suddenly appeared in massive quantities on the London market, gin (geneva) from Holland being the most popular because the cheapest, but also whiskey from Ireland and Scotland and brandy from France. In London special spirit bars sprang up almost overnight and in vast numbers. There is a story of one gin bar advertising: "Drunk one penny. Dead drunk twopence. Straw free."

Spirit drinking, above all in London, became a very real national crisis. By 1732, London, with a population of well under one million, had 15,500 drinking places, or approximately one for every fifty of the population, and half of these were spirit bars. In 1736 the Gin Act was passed, requiring an annual fifty-pound license fee from the publican and a tax of one pound per gallon on spirits. It was an immediate failure, for bootlegging and illegal drinking places spread on an enormous scale.

Speaking in the House of Lords in 1743, Lord Lonsdale described the condition of London in the following words:

> In every part of this great metropolis whoever shall pass along the streets will find wretchedness stretched upon the pavement, insensible and motionless, and only removed by the charity of passengers from the danger of being crushed by carriages or trampled by horses or strangled with filth in the common sewers . . . These liquors not only infatuate the mind

but poison the body; they not only fill our streets with madness and our prisons with criminals, but our hospitals with cripples . . . Those women who riot in this poisonous debauchery are quickly disabled from bearing children, or produce children diseased from their birth.

This was not the normal condition throughout the eighteenth century: as a result of the failure of the 1736 act virtually all licenses and taxes had been abolished in 1742. A new form of licensing was introduced in 1753, concerned primarily with landlords, who now had to give character references, in the country largely supplied by the clergy, to obtain a license. An import duty was reintroduced on spirits, but again with little effect. However in the nineteenth century the liquor situation gradually became rationalized, with one severe setback. In 1825 the tax on spirits was lowered from twelve to seven shillings per gallon. At that time half the spirits consumed were bootleg, and it was realized that drastic taxation always brought this about. Henceforth taxation was increased gradually, but steadily. First introduced in 1660 on the manufacture of spirits and beer, by 1909 it had amounted to 30 per cent of the internal revenue: * by then a mass of taxes on distributors, wholesalers, and the publicans themselves had gradually made drunkenness too costly for the general public.

Licensing hours were introduced, children forbidden, the use of pubs as houses of prostitution abolished. Increased penalties for drunkenness were introduced more than once and "drunk and disorderly" became a serious offense. By the First World War the English public-drinking system had more or less settled down to what it has remained, though licensing hours have since been shortened and the cost of drink has gone up over 1,000 per cent, but the ratio of one large whiskey to one pint of beer has remained approximately the same, as have the strengths, and the real cost of drink has remained more or less static in view of inflation.

* In 1909, income tax in Britain was, by our standards, negligible. At the time of writing the total income that the U. K. Exchequer derives from the various drink taxes is estimated at 5 per cent of the government's entire income; in Ireland at 13 per cent; in the U.S.A. it is not available, owing to the high variations in state taxes.

It is often asked why prohibition was never attempted in Britain and also whether licensing laws effectively diminish the consumption of alcohol.

The answer to the first question is essentially political. In England the temperance movement never had the force of its American equivalent. There is no written constitution to be amended, and any British government that imposed prohibition would almost certainly be thrown out by the next general election. In Wales, on the other hand, and in Scotland—or at least in parts of those provinces—the Low Churches, always the most powerful supporters of anti-drink legislation, predominate and have succeeded in imposing stricter licensing laws, in particular as regards Sunday drinking. Finally, in Britain as a whole the government could not afford to lose the vast taxation revenue which it derives from the liquor trade and manufacture.

As for the licensing laws, it is probable that they do have a marginal effect on the consumption of alcohol, though not by drink-searching alcoholics or even determined heavy drinkers, who can find ways of circumventing them, such as afternoon clubs or nightclubs. The somewhat distasteful spectacle of drink-gulping as the publican calls "last orders, please" is more than compensated for by the absence of drunks in the streets at all hours of the night. Furthermore, the table given as Appendix III does show that the countries with the highest consumption do not have licensing laws, but certainly this is not a major factor.

The Australian licensing laws used to be remarkable. So heavy was the liquor consumption that an attempt at semi-prohibition was introduced by closing the pubs at 6 P.M. The logic was that this is the hour when most people start drinking. The result was the "six-o'clock swill," which speaks for itself. Even moderate Australian drinkers would drink as much as they wanted before six. So would heavy drinkers, and it is obviously worse from every point of view to be drunk all evening than just before bedtime. Much Australian alcoholism can be attributed to the "six-o'clock swill," which has now been abolished by more sensible legislation.

Endogenous depression is a term already used, and it will recur frequently when we come to discussing the disease syndrome attitude toward alcoholism later in this book. Endogenous depression, unlike the reactive variety, needs no outside stimulus, but will probably be aggravated by such. You may laugh it off, you may lose it when you lose yourself in work, perhaps, or in love or in the contemplation of beauty, but it will still be there *underneath*. Drink will not destroy it: indeed quite the contrary, it will usually bring out the evil side of what, in highly abbreviated form, is often called the Jungian shadow persona. It is, in fact, simply a new and fanciful word for melancholia, invented quite recently by the medical scientists to act as an antithesis, or at least as a condition quite divorced from, reactive depression. A melancholic is usually born such, though there seem to be cases where this condition can be acquired. King Henry I, whose only son was drowned in the White Ship and who "never smiled again," may have been melancholic before—we know little about that King of England—but he may have become such. Therefore endogenous depression may or may not be hereditary.

The drink you take to "cheer you up" when you find you have lost your fountain pen, i.e., to dispel reactive depression, is multiplied by the endogenously depressed man into the scores or hundreds of bottles that culminate in the alcoholic disease or diseased condition. Yet it is somehow hard to believe that all those men and women whom Lord Lonsdale saw lying in the gutter were born acute melancholics, though some undoubtedly were.

Then there are at least two global conditions that produce melancholia over the generations, so that it is hard to say whether it is hereditary or environmental in origin, though Darwin and his followers have taught us at much greater length than this that environment and mutation may change heredity, while political and economic history have in some measure denied this. The removal of the first contributary factor in melancholia, political or economic misery, may simply shift the weight of drinking to another class of person: in England and America today to the newly affluent youth. This will be explored more fully later in this book.

The second non-individual factor is climate. There is no more reason to feel depressed in Norway than in Provence, yet the extent of melancholia in northern climates is evident in their greatest literature (with of course many exceptions), while in

Europe the line that separates wine drinkers in the south from beer and spirit drinkers in the north is even evident in the greatest painting. Again with exceptions, there is little gaiety in the great painters of the German-Dutch school but much in the work of their Italian peers where the sunlight keeps pouring in. This is not in any way a comparison of talent, but rather of mood, and the greatest artist imparts his moods. I can only speak for myself: a Rembrandt or a Dürer will not give me the gaiety of a Botticelli or a Cellini. Classical Greek architecture is one great paean of praise, praise of the Gods and of the skies. In what was to become Protestant northern man, God is in the heart of that man, and the great cathedrals with their stained-glass windows are His fortresses against Evil.

The Russians drink beer and vodka, and in very large quantities. Writing of Turgenev in 1881, an author said that he ". . . lifted the veil which covered this queer, quaint, stupefied people. He spoke to us of its deep alcoholism, of its benumbed, inactive conscience, of its ignorance of liberty." I understand that alcoholism remains a very severe problem in Soviet Russia, while the rest of the quotation speaks for itself.

Almost as early as Britain, Norway and Sweden had to take fairly drastic action against alcoholism, and parts of both countries were declared "dry" by law. Prussia, too, was subject to alcoholism, but this was controlled from an early stage. In the old Austro-Hungarian Empire, alcoholism was little trouble save in its northern extremities, in what is now southern Poland, where special laws had to be passed, and it has already been commented on that the French noticed the drunkenness of their immigrant Polish miners.

Statistical comparisons between countries are misleading, since no two nations compile their statistics from the same bases and sources, but the United Kingdom of 1800–1922 was a unit. Its statistics show that, London apart, drinking grew heavier as one moved westward, into wetter weather and, incidentally, into a more Gaelic population. And Ireland was far the most drunken part of the U.K. To this it must be added that it was the poorest, most oppressed, and worst governed portion of the kingdom, and had been for centuries. Indeed everywhere, from Brittany to the Hebrides, the Celtic-speaking (or recently Celtic-speaking) peoples are the fragmented remnants of a once great power. Defeat produces misery and poverty—and melancholia. But here we are speaking of climate. I quote from J. M. Synge's little known masterpiece *In Wicklow and West Kerry*. The essay of which these are the opening paragraphs is called "The Oppression of the Hills."

Among the cottages that are scattered through the hills of County Wicklow I have met with many people who show in a singular way the influence of a particular locality. These people live for the most part beside old roads and pathways where hardly one man passes in the day, and look out all the year on unbroken barriers of heath. At every season heavy rains fall for often a week at a time, till the thatch drips with water stained to a dull chestnut, and the floor in the cottages seems to be going back to the condition of the bogs near it. Then the clouds break, and there is a night of terrific storm from the south-west—all the larches that survive in these places are bowed and twisted towards the point where the sun rises in June—when the winds come down through the narrow glens with the congested whirl and roar of a torrent, breaking at times for sudden moments of silence that keep up the tension of the mind. At such times the people crouch all night over a few sods of turf, and the dogs howl in the lanes.

When the sun rises there is a morning of almost supernatural radiance, and even the oldest men and women come out into the air with the joy of children who have recovered from a fever. In the evening it is raining again. This peculiar climate, acting on a population that is already lonely and dwindling, has caused or increased a tendency to nervous depression among the people, and every degree of sadness, from that of the man who is merely mournful to that of the man who has spent half his life in the madhouse, is common among these hills.

And the man who has spent half of his life in the madhouse was often immured because his endogenous and reactive depression had driven him into alcoholism. For Synge was writing in the first decade of this century.

CHAPTER XII

Sin and Shame in America

Almost all the great religions have been hostile to drink and above all to drunkenness. In China the Confucian heritage has left a sensation of contempt for insobriety, which endures and which is why the Chinese drink little. Hinduism and Islam are totally prohibitionist. The Christian attitude is more tolerant, but every revivalist movement since Calvin and before has been hostile, often violently so. An attempted compromise was found in the word temperance, but in the drink context it rapidly lost its real meaning of moderate drinking and was used to mean merely total abstention. The members of the Temperance Society, one of the earliest founded in America, at Saratoga in 1808, would have looked askance even at the "social drinker" described earlier.

Why did temperance societies flourish so in the United States? (By 1833 there were some six thousand such societies, with a membership of more than one million. They flourished in England as well, under the early patronage of the young Queen Victoria.) Some broad generalizations are needed here concerning American history in the context of alcoholism.

In colonial times the dominant but not the only strain along the eastern border, between the French in Quebec and the Spaniards in Florida, was English, or to be more exact British. Jamestown was founded in 1607, Plymouth in 1620, and the Massachusetts Bay Colony in 1629. These original colonists were not penniless emigrants, but what would now be called members of the lower middle class, primarily yeomen farmers financed by London merchants, the farmers in search of land, the merchants of profits. The Dutch were established in their colony—New York and New Jersey—but were forced to surrender this to the

English in 1664. William Penn organized the Quaker enclaves south of New York into a colony, Pennsylvania, in 1681. Shortly after the Revocation of the Edict of Nantes in 1685 fairly large numbers of French Huguenots arrived in America. Extremist German sects, such as the Amish, also crossed the Atlantic, as did many Welsh non-conformists. The Dutch created large estates. In the South two crops, tobacco and cotton, replaced general farming, and slavery was introduced on a large scale to work what were often quasi-aristocratic domains. The first slaves were brought to what is now the United States by the Dutch in the 1620s. Early in the eighteenth century clearances began on a large scale in England and, even more, in Northern Ireland. Great numbers of Scotch-Irish moved to America, principally Pennsylvania and the South. But the New Englanders retained their original motive, yeoman farming, and it was they who pushed the Indians of the North steadily westward in search of land for younger sons. The Scotch-Irish were the principal pioneers farther south, who treated the Indians with the same rough justice that their forebears had used against the native Irish. Cities were small in colonial times and there were few "mechanics" in America, manufactured goods and even good clothing being imported from England.

It is a myth that New England was founded as a refuge for Puritans, as Pennsylvania was for Quakers, but there was a strong Puritan element, though the Church of England remained, until the Revolution, the state church, the King of England at its head. An attempt at a Puritan Congregationalist takeover in 1634 in Massachusetts and the establishment, presumably, of a theocracy was thwarted. Meanwhile the Anglican Church was forced to share power with an elected assembly, though only church members might vote. In effect, therefore, from the very beginning the intermixture of church and state was far greater than even the Tudors had achieved in England, where the Church since Cranmer had had very little real political power. Even its moral power declined steadily until today it is almost nonexistent.

And in all America, with the exception of the Anglicans, who after the Revolution were called Episcopalians, the churches were "low," whether of Dutch, French, English, or Scotch-Irish origin. The Scotch-Irish, and even more so the New Englanders, carried their Calvinist morality westward. What is now called the Midwest was inbred with this morality. It was the religion taught to the slaves and in many cases to the Indians. It has undoubtedly remained the basic morality of the Americans to this day. American popular reaction to Watergate was a clear-cut example of that rather simple morality in action.

We have been taught that the eighteenth century produced the Age of Enlightenment, with its power plant in the Paris of the Encyclopedia. But it was also the age of religious revivalism, which in America was called the Age of the Awakening, and which lasted for some fifty years, roughly from 1725. Among its instigators was a certain Jonathan Edwards, who was born in 1703 (the same year John Wesley was born in England), who became President of the College of New Jersey (now Princeton), and died in 1758. To judge by his own sermons and writings, he was a most unattractive but obviously impressive figure. It would be no exaggeration to say that he was more Calvinist than Knox or Calvin himself. For example, he foresaw the blessed in heaven enjoying the spectacle of the damned being tortured by the fiends in hell. And only the uttermost self-control, helped a bit by the grace of God, could offer even the prospect of a passport to heaven.

His successors were on the whole less extreme but at times even more eccentric. All believed in the sinfulness of drink and of fornication. Partly as a result of the disestablishment and general decline of the Anglican Church in favor of the more puritan Congregationalists, and partly because of the explosive nature of all revolutions, a mass of new, small sects appeared upon the scene during the period between the Revolution and about 1840, a time that saw relatively few new immigrants arrive, a time when America was really built and the major reforms of President Andrew Jackson firmly created the property-owning democracy that has endured. This period also saw the growth of the cities and the introduction of industrialism on a large scale, particularly in the North and what is now the Midwest. Industrialization meant the amassing of capital and the creation of a large class of industrial workers who were soon coming with the vast immigrations.

Some of the sects were so eccentric that they were forced to migrate westward. The most famous of these were the Mormons, who regarded property as the root of all evil, and who therefore practiced not only a form of economic communism but also abolished marriage in favor of polygamy and polyandry, a not altogether happy experiment, later abandoned. The majority of the other sects largely merged to form the Baptists. For both Mormons and Baptists, total abstinence from alcohol was a basic law. Among the Calvinist sects, abolition of slavery also became a popular cause.

Drinking to excess thus became, for the mass of Americans, a sin, and to indulge in drink a matter of shame. Local attempts to make the selling of alcohol illegal, on the other hand, were generally a failure and American pragmatism usually led to their fairly rapid abandonment, for one of the very fundamentals of the American ethos was that government, whether federal, state, or regional, should not interfere in the life of the individual.

However, from the first landings on Plymouth Rock to the arrival of the first covered wagon convoys in California, the Americans on the move had to create, by force of circumstances, small, self-reliant communities of pioneers. Drunkenness and adultery could quickly cause the dissolution of these voluntary and temporary communities, with catastrophe to all. On the one hand, therefore, this reinforced the endeavors of the religious sects to prevent alcoholism and fornication; on the other, it left a heritage of egalitarian "neighborliness" that has endured in rural and small-town communities. To this day Americans have a tendency to complain of the "impersonality" of life in the big cities, a complaint that is heard far less often from Londoners or Parisians. When a dozen caravans rolled westward, everybody knew what everyone in the other caravans was doing. If a man, or less often a woman, wanted a drink, he would probably take it in secret and perhaps in shame.

The outriders, as it were, of these small communities had a very different morality. They were, first, the trappers. Later when the Great Plains were opened, they were the cowboys who would drive the cattle for a thousand miles, from the extreme Southwest to the stockyards of Chicago. They were the gold rush miners of 1849 and, after the Civil War, many veterans of the

Confederate armies, in search of a livelihood. From their ranks
were recruited the celebrated badmen of the West, Jesse James
and his like. They were also men who could not fit into the Low
Church communities that spread quite quickly across the continent. We know them only too well from the movies and TV, because they became in a curious way the folk heroes of American
legend, the Robin Hoods of the New World. Tough, swaggering,
hard-drinking, hard-riding, virile, quick on the draw, Indian
killers, they have been imbued with a certain glamour which
they can seldom have possessed.

It is said that the Dutch first sold guns and alcohol to the Indians, and when Peter Stuyvesant ruled the New Netherlands,
his orders forbidding such sales were ignored. The badmen, in
particular the Scotch-Irish who were seldom without their pot
stills, made a steady profit on such sales ahead of the true
pioneer groups. And when these groups settled down into little
communities, they too were on occasion plundered, though the
badmen preferred to hold up single coaches, in particular, of
course, those carrying money. But then are not Dick Turpin and
the other glamorized highwaymen in some measure folk heroes
in England?

These little communities must have been bleak places, offering
no form of entertainment whatsoever save the saloon, which we
also know so well from TV, dreary, probably dirty places in
which to get drunk. And to these the men would gravitate, and
drink, and sometimes fight. It was then that the legend of the
tough hombre was dreamed up. They could feel, with Mark
Twain's *Huckleberry Finn*, that it would be good "to light out
for the territory ahead of the rest, because Aunt Sally she's going
to adopt me, and civilize me, and I can't stand it. I been there
before."

Indeed, that is precisely what thousands of Aunt Sallys were
doing throughout the nineteenth century. As the caravans rolled
westward and the new communities were hewn out of forest and
wilderness, the women had to work as hard as the men, often
doing the same work, as well as keeping the house once it was
built and raising large families. American women had done this
from the beginning, and they acquired a status which they had
thoroughly earned and which, in general, they have never lost.

Alexis de Tocqueville, who visited America early in the century, spoke with admiration of the confidence and self-assurance of American women, and ascribed the strength of American civilization largely to them.

It is therefore hardly surprising that they disliked the saloons. Even before the Civil War, Midwestern housewives physically attacked and often destroyed the bars where their husbands got drunk.

The women's pressure was probably more effective in the long run than a huge anti-drink publicity campaign that had first been launched by the American Temperance Society, founded in 1808. I quote at length from *The Americans* by J. C. Furnas:

The catchword *Temperance* had not been too ironical. Its approaching perversion was implicit, in what is usually taken as its practical birth in 1808. A country doctor, Billy James Clark, practising near Saratoga, New York—a fateful area—read Rush's *Inquiry* and burst in on the local parson announcing: "We shall all become a community of drunkards in this town unless something is done to arrest the progress of intemperance." The pioneer Temperance society, then and there founded, pledged its members wholly to abstain from hard liquor but allowed wine at public dinners, as a sort of social duty. That went farther than what Rush had had in mind. It gaspingly assumed that at least a large majority of persons exposing themselves to hard liquor are doomed to be degenerating drunkards.

The actual odds are nothing like so high, of course, even among daily drinkers. That was clear all through American life at the time. It was the British visitor's standard observation that though most Americans were steady tipplers, disabling inebriety was seldom seen. ". . . many of them," said a witness in 1818, "drink [spirits] almost the moment after they get out of bed, and also at frequent intervals during the day; but . . . excessive drinking is rare." In 1828 Captain Basil Hall marvelled that this "universal practice of sipping a little at a time, but frequently . . . [every] half an hour to a couple of hours, during the whole day" produced so little overt drunkenness. But commonsense fact seldom meant much to the kinds of

parsons and pamphleteers then urging on the Temperance
movement. Their craving for viewing with alarm led them to
most intemperate statements. In 1811 the Reverend Nathaniel
Prime of Long Island maintained that "drunkenness and lewd-
ness go hand in hand . . . few who have drunk a gill [four
ounces] of ardent spirits can be exposed to . . . small temptation without becoming adulterous in the sight of God." The
Reverend Dr. Heman Humphrey, mainstay of Amherst College, warned that "All who embark on this flood [of spirits
drinking] are in danger of hell fire." By 1821 the Reverend
Dr. Lyman Beecher, never a man to keep his oar out, was
lending his prestige to the contention that ". . . no man can
use [spirits] prudently or without mocking God can pray . . .
'lead us not into temptation.'"

That substituted a nursery-style Mustn't Touch for mature
self-control in the use of spirits. On that crude basis was
created the vigorous national American Temperance Society
modelled, like so many American reforms, on the propaganda
machines that had moved Britain to outlaw first the overseas
slave trade and then slavery in the West Indies. This array of
foes of Rum, many also deep in other reforms, claimed
8,000-odd local branches set up in all but two states, more
than 1,500,000 members pledged to eschew spirits and 4,000
distilleries put out of business—not an absurd figure, for the
small local distillery was often as much a part of a new settle-
ment as the tannery. And the official meaning of Temperance
had been unscrupulously established as: "the moderate and
proper use of things beneficial; and abstinence from things
hurtful. Ardent spirits being . . . poison . . . and . . . the
grand means of intoxication, [we pledge to] abstain from the
drinking and . . . furnishing of [spirits] and [to try] to induce
the whole community to do the same." That is, temperance, a
discretionary virtue of deservedly high repute, was now lending its prestige to Temperance, a self-righteous taboo.

Temporarily the righteous had forgotten that the old children of Israel knew not distilling and that, according to their
Bibles, it was wine, not spirits, that led Noah and Lot to behave so scandalously. The omission was to plague them sore.

Not only were lower-class drunkards not disappearing—
another generation of them stepped gamely up to replace their
Rum-killed elders—but it was soon plain that to identify hard
stuff as prime villain was to ignore the shattered cider-drunk, a
standard object in the rural landscape, and the overconvivial
Quality always demonstrating that one can get falling-down
drunk on fine old Madeira. Temperance leaders on the local
level began to use a New Pledge binding the taker to total abstinence from anything detectably alcoholic—that is, from
wine, cider, beer . . . "Taste not, touch not, handle not" was
the slogan of this extension of the taboo so sweeping that it
came to apply even to the use of wines and brandy to flavour
cooking. To justify the New Pledge, one now had to exagger-
ate the risks of degenerate alcoholism lurking in any acquaintance with alcohol. T. S. Arthur, author of *Ten Nights in
a Bar-room*, which, as novel and then stage play, did for Temperance what *Uncle Tom's Cabin* did for abolitionism, wrote
that "for every [moderate drinker] who restrains himself, ten
will rush on to ruin." A Methodist circuit rider's sermons wandered still farther from sense in "I never knew a man . . . in
the habit of drinking regularly that did not become a drunkard."

The persistence of millions of regular drinkers who did not
exemplify Temperance propaganda by becoming drunkards
was exasperating. This led the zealot to denounce the genuine
moderate drinker as savagely as if he had been a distiller or a
barkeep. Thomas S. Grimké, intellectual reformer and elder
brother of the famous sisters, laid it down that "Temperate
drinkers are the parents of all the drunkards who dishonour
and afflict our country." Gerrit Smith, as hot against Rum as he
was against slavery and for Bloomers, told the U. S. House of
Representatives: "I would that no person were able to drink
intoxicating liquors without immediately becoming a drunkard." Such extreme doctrine troubled many staider members of
the American Temperance Society and its broad successor, the
American Temperance Union. In 1836 it adopted the New
Pledge but only after a divisive fight. This dissension, coupled
with others over divorcing Temperance from antislaveryism

and over whether to enlist law against Rum, cost the movement much momentum. And after the panic of 1837 men in
broadcloth were disinclined to dig deep into their pockets for
the cost of Temperance's printing and propaganda agents.

Actually Temperance, like abolitionism a few years earlier,
was about to shift base. Initiative was now to come not from
the top down but from the bottom up—from the gutter, in
fact. So far the purpose had been largely what Dr. Clark had
envisaged—to keep normal persons from becoming drunkards.
Drunkards themselves were either denounced as loathsomely
hopeless or patronized as horrible examples. Now, filling the
partial vacuum left by loss of zeal among the Quality, alcoholics among the lower orders seized the stage in a sort of
Drunkards-of-the-World-Unite! frame of mind, proclaiming a
new gospel of self-rehabilitation. It began in the 1830s as
drink-bedevilled wageworkers in Boston, New York City, Phil-
adelphia and Baltimore got together to take the New Pledge
and—much more important—help one another keep it while
persuading other alcoholics to come and do likewise. The Boston group's grasp of the issues was sounder than Rush's or
Clark's. "FRIENDS," read their manifesto, "you are wretched
. . . You can have no peace here, and no peace hereafter . . .
we were once drunkards. We are now happy, our wives are
comfortable; our children are provided for; we are in better
health . . . we now drink . . . no kind of intoxicating liquor.
There is no safety for you nor for us, but in giving it up entirely. Come then, ye drunkards . . . cast off the fetters of intemperance, and forever determine to be free." This contention that many abject alcoholics could be salvaged by total
abstinence was new among Temperance men. So was this
spontaneity independent of leadership from their social supe-
riors.

By 1840 these stirrings had flowered into the Washingtonian
movement that swept the nation. Its founders were craftsmen—
a tailor, a carpenter, two blacksmiths, a silversmith and a
coachmaker—who all drank too much too often in a Baltimore
tavern. In fun they sent two of their number to a Temperance
lecture. They returned uneasily impressed, and the upshot was

the Washington Temperance Society, a mutual-support teetotalers' club based on the new pledge. At weekly meetings they
rose to tell outsider guests, potential members threatened by
alcoholism, how far down drink had dragged them before they
won free and how much better their and their families' lives
were now that the Demon had been sent packing. As the six
founders developed skill as down-to-earth platform missionaries, the number of their newly vitalized members grew
toward 1,000. The analogy to today's Alcoholics Anonymous is
strong. So is that to the "experience" sessions at the camp
meetings of the time, where the saved described their past sins
and present happiness to attract the waverers. But the early
Washingtonians, unlike AA, renounced prayer and other religious props for staunchness. They also declined to follow the
conventional Temperance zeal in denouncing saloon-keepers
as callous tools of the Devil, pointing out instead that no law
forced anybody into a saloon in the first place.

The Washingtonians originally limited their membership to
those with gnawing drink problems. As their numbers grew,
however, attracting wide attention, they began to admit well-
meaning admirers and tended to become a pledge-signing society of the old kind. This was encouraged by the brilliant
platform performances of an early recruit, English-born John
H. W. Hawkins, a drink-shattered hatter, who was soon making a career of spreading the Washingtonian good word in the
Northeastern states. Membership spread from Maryland to
Maine and westward to the Mississippi. Abraham Lincoln,
hardly a drinker at all, was one of hundreds of thousands join-
ing as a morally healthy gesture. There was a ladies' auxiliary,
the Martha Washingtons. There were Washingtonian parades
stiff with transparencies and floats extolling the virtues of pure
cold water and dramatizing the perils of Rum in symbols such
as snakes and devils. It was showy, but it meant dilution of the
steely zeal of the original self-rescued band of brothers keeping their eyes firmly on the realities of alcoholism. Presently
Hawkins was calling for resort to law ("Moral suasion for the
unfortunate drunkard, and legal suasion for the drunkard-
MAKER") and abusing barkeeps ("You might as well talk

about a pious devil, a virtuous prostitute, or an honest thief as
to talk about a rumseller . . . having 'a good moral character.'") He also took up religion, even obtaining ordination
as a Methodist minister.

Thus spreading itself too thin, Washingtonianism frayed and
came apart. But it had handed Temperance over to the people,
and out of its ruins came another popular movement in the
shape of solemnly teetotaling fraternal orders. Veterans of the
Washingtonian wars organized the first outstanding one, the
Order of the Sons of Temperance, which added to teetotaling
the lodge-style features of sickness and death benefits. By 1850
the Sons had enrolled some 200,000 members—a success imi-
tated by the Order of Templars of Honor and Temperance, the
National Temple of Honor, the Society of Good Samaritans,
the Independent Order of Good Templars . . . The last eventually outstripped the Sons and even spread to Europe. All
had secret meetings under guard, grips, passwords, officers' ti-
tles of the Most Worshipful and Worthy Potentate sort. Few
civic parades were complete without the Sons or the Good
Templars or both marching sweatily under their gaudily
embroidered trappings of mystic meaning, the band playing
some such Temperance war song as "Away the Bowl." or:

> No matter what anyone says, no matter what anyone
> thinks,
> If you want to be happy the rest of your life
> Don't marry a man if he drinks!

After them probably marched the local children's Cold
Water Army piping something similar under charge of solici-
tous Sunday-school teachers of both sexes. For as the Civil
War approached, Temperance's presumptions and propaganda
sprayed over most American institutions. Squibs and bits of
verse denouncing Rum had long been tucked into the ubiqui-
tous almanacs. Succeeding editions of the blue-backed
Webster's Speller had taken to occasional anti-Rum essays
about the cost of tippling and its physical effects. There were
Temperance novels by the score, Temperance newspapers and
song recitals. Temperance plays infiltrated the basically
wicked stage. Acceptance by repertory companies came not

only to *Ten Nights* but also to its predecessor, *The Drunkard,* and to *The Bottle,* an imported adaptation to the stage of the material in the temperance engravings of George Cruikshank, the highly popular English illustrator.

There were Temperance hotels—mostly bad, as even Temperance men admitted—Temperance steamboats and canal packets, Temperance merchant ships much approved of by underwriters. The U.S. armed forces severely abolished or commuted the morning ration of spirits. There were two successive Congressional Temperance societies—badly needed, too, for the heavy perfume wafting up from the legislative chambers was a good third Old Monongahela rye, the other two ingredients being chewing tobacco and unbathed statesman. One of the noisiest I-was-a-drunkard-but-no-longer-thank-God Temperance spellbinders trouping the land was Thomas F. Marshall, Congressman from Kentucky, never more eloquent against Rum than when stumbling drunk. The most striking example cited *in terrorem* was Edward A. Hannegan, Congressman from Indiana, who wound up an alcoholic career by the drunken murder of his brother-in-law.

The Civil War, like all wars, caused a great deal of drinking, and the Temperance movement withdrew from the limelight. It was not, however, abandoned. In the 1870s the women returned to the fight, with redoubled vigor. I quote once again from J. C. Furnas:

Its godfather was Dr. Dio Lewis, the eminent apostle of Temperance, righteous diet and calisthenics, one of whose repertory of lectures was "The Influence of Christian Women in the Temperance Cause." Much of it consisted of the story of his dear old mother in New York State, cursed with an alcoholic spouse, who had summoned the godliest women of the local church and led them, praying and singing hymns, into the local saloon to bid the startled owner in God's name to close down, which, after a doomed struggle against their tireless spiritual ministrations, he consented to do, Glory hallelujah! and on into a rhapsody on what women got together with God's blessing could accomplish.

As Lewis lectured his way through the land late in 1873, he got warm hearings for his mother's prowess. Finally in Fredonia, New York, in the far western tip of the state, his plea to the women in his audience to follow the late Mrs. Lewis' example brought 100 of them to their feet with their husbands pledging support, and the next morning, led by a judge's wife and a minister's wife, "revered matrons as well as young ladies", they poured into the local hotel barroom. Denying that he ever drank himself, the terrified principal partner promised to stop selling drink if the ladies would make the druggist across the street do the same. By nightfall they had brought the druggist to his knees. Lewis went on to spread the flames to Jamestown, the county seat; there 50 women were soon on the prowl and bar after bar was closing. In southwestern Ohio, where his bookings next took him, they kindled such a blaze that it spread spontaneously. In Hillsboro, seat of a county founded by high-chinned Virginians accustomed to setting influential local examples, the lady leader was the wife of a judge and a daughter of an early governor of the state. "Let us proceed to our sacred mission trusting in the God of Jacob!" were the words with which she mustered her storming party of lady Methodists, Baptists, Presbyterians and Quakers—Episcopalians and Catholics were usually less zealous about the war on Rum—and led them against saloonkeepers and druggists.

The tone was sweetly imperious. The first saloonkeeper to resist was told: "We have come not to threaten, nor even to upbraid; but in the name of our Heavenly Friend and Saviour and in His spirit to forgive and to commend you to His pardon if you will abandon a business . . . so damaging to our hearts and homes . . . Let us pray!" When a rescusant locked the barroom door to prevent a sort of kneel-in, the second most august matron in town knelt on the top doorstep and prayed at him through the keyhole until he knuckled under. In December slush and snow the ladies knelt around saloon doors in an immobile picketing that forced the customers to be prayed at on their way in, which often spoiled the flavor of the drinks inside. "Passers-by uncovered their heads," wrote an eyewitness for the religious press. ". . . not a man who saw them kneeling there but felt that if he were entering heaven's gate and if one of these women were to approach, he would . . . let her enter first." As the weather worsened, the ladies' menfolk provided a roofed, three-sided shelter with a small stove in which they could in comparative comfort beleaguer John Barleycorn. When a Rum seller surrendered and went out of business, the ladies saw to it that he got fair value at the sale of his fixtures, glassware and so on, often bid on things themselves, in fact, to be long preserved as mementos of when mother was a heroine. The silver-mounted gavel with which Frances Willard kept conventions of the Woman's Christian Temperance Union in order is said to have been a bung starter thus acquired from a Hillsboro bar.

Eastward into Pennsylvania, northwestward into Illinois and Michigan, scores of sizable towns now saw what the newspapers were calling the Women's Crusade. Only in the large cities—Cincinnati, Cleveland, Pittsburgh—did the authorities do much to discourage it, in spite of the dictum of an Indiana judge that "Mob law enforced by women is no better than mob law enforced by men." For in smaller places the authorities were well aware that the embattled ladies were egged on or at least not frowned on by the powers behind the scenes in the community. Their menfolk were usually the local bankers, ministers, merchants, large property owners. The saloonkeeper recognizing among the crowd of bonnet-and-shawled self-righteousness in his barroom the wife of the banker who held his mortgage, the wife of the lumber and coal dealer to whom he owed $653, the mother of the county attorney and the daughter of his family doctor was unlikely too roughly to resist their holy bullying. Only a small minority of the assailed threw water on the ladies or put pepper on the hot stove to make them sneeze. Besides, there was the American taboo on shoving a lady, which the crusaders exploited with the aplomb of skilled blackmailers. They had always known in their bones that they were the morally superior sex, endowed by their Creator with privileges to match. See how these brutal, hulking barkeeps quailed before pure womanhood while the male lords of creation merely stood on the other side of the street admiring their women for doing what men could never have done without provoking violence and the law—even had they had the spunk and imagination to try.

Several states briefly went dry: Maine, for example, in 1851 and Iowa in 1894. In all cases save Kansas, which has remained dry to this day, bootlegging and speakeasies almost immediately made the drink problem so bad that Prohibition was repealed. This, however, did not prevent the first formation of a national Prohibition Party in 1865.

Nor did direct action die out at once. At the turn of the century the celebrated Carry Nation was, between arrests, smashing saloons with a small hatchet. However, she was regarded as a freak if not a psychopath. Yet in the totally altered circumstances of industrialized America, with its millions of Irish, Italian, German, Hungarian, Polish, Russian, and Jewish immigrants, the ideal of prohibition continued to grow throughout the opening years of the twentieth century. For a vote against liquor remained a vote against sin.

CHAPTER XIII

Prohibition and Psychoanalysis

The 1920s brought two novelties to the United States of America, prohibition and psychoanalysis, the one a native product, the other an importation. Freud, whose *Interpretation of Dreams* had first been published in 1900 but remained unread even in his native Vienna for several years, had in fact first visited America in 1909, where he had lectured at Clark University, but his theories did not percolate down from advanced medical circles into the mass culture of the bourgeoisie for another decade and more. Prohibition had much deeper roots, as has been shown in the last chapter.

The story of the introduction of Prohibition (the Eighteenth Amendment to the Constitution of the United States, also known as the Volstead Act) when it was voted on in Congress drew the necessary support in a sometimes underhand way. The story is too complicated to tell here in any but the most superficial detail. The women's temperance movements (the Woman's Christian Temperance Union, or WCTU, being the largest) had never dropped their stand against drink. After about 1900, however, they had embraced a number of other good causes, such as the abolition of prostitution and, above all, emancipation for themselves. Their progress in this cause of votes for women, already enacted by 1896 in the states of Wyoming, Utah, Colorado, and Idaho, paralleled that of the suffragettes in England, with whom they were in close contact. By about 1910 this had really become the dominant cause of the WCTU, and in 1920 they triumphed with the Nineteenth Amendment. But while they were engaged in this struggle, their attention had somewhat wandered from temperance, and though they continued to give that cause their full support, other forces had moved in and taken charge.

In the 1890s the Prohibition Party was functioning. Apart from what its name implies, it was basically apolitical. It was never very large, perhaps some 5 per cent of the voting population. It had an essentially democratic attitude, though it never had a hope of ever gaining its ends through democratic means. The people of America continued to vote Republican or Democrat. Very rarely in this century has a third party stood a chance. With its left-wing, Fabian bias, the Prohibition Party might have competed with the two other great parties, had the Americans felt any more attraction to socialism than they did to prohibitionism. But the very fact that it had a moderately wide program made its appeal to many of the drys weaker.

Far more powerful was the Anti-Saloon League. Founded in Ohio in 1893, it soon spread thinly across the nation, particularly in country districts. Its founder was a Congregationalist, a hot-gospeler and orator of power. It was tightly authoritarian and did not make the mistake of the WCTU or of the Prohibition Party in espousing other good causes. It existed solely to close the saloons. At every local, state, or federal election its members were ordered to vote for the candidate who was dry and who endorsed the closing of the saloons. If there were no such candidate, its members might vote Democrat or Republican as they chose. The League did not aspire to be itself a political party, nor in its early days did it advocate national Prohibition as such, save insofar as this should automatically close the saloons. In close elections—and many elections in most of America are very close—the switching of a few thousand or even a few hundred votes one way or the other could and can determine the result. Further, the members of the League did go to the polling booths, whereas nearly half the electorate seldom bothered.

The League was a movement, a *Bewegung*, rather than a political party. It acquired what might be called, in an American context, protofascist tendencies. The corner saloon was a smelly, unattractive place, virtually off limits to the members of the great non-conformist churches of native American stock. It was depicted as filled with foreigners, specifically Irishmen engaged in their dirty political maneuvers, but also with other foreign-born industrial workers. Many of the barkeeps were German-born. Thus was xenophobia introduced. The League appealed to the countryman against the immoral inhabitants of the big cities, some of whom were indeed bums. In the South it appealed to the rednecks, on the grounds that the less liquor the black man had the less dangerous would he be to the whites and particularly to their women. It had an anti-Catholic tinge and ignored the temperance units set up by the Roman clergy, for it clung to the greater respectability of the Baptists and Congregationalists. It does not appear to have been anti-Semitic, but then Jews did not drink much and were scarcely prominent in the corner saloon.

Some states were already dry. Indeed state and regional prohibition had been tried, with a marked lack of success, since the 1840s. In 1913 the Anti-Saloon League won its first national victory with the Webb-Kenyon Act, which forbade the passing of liquor from a wet state to a dry one. This of course necessitated an increase of skill on the part of the bootlegger, who had first learned his trade in the dry states. It also increased the amount of home distillery, hooch, poteen, moonshine, bathtub gin, call it what you will, in the dry states themselves.

Elated by this success, the Anti-Saloon League now reversed its tactical program and stole the clothes of the failed Prohibition Party. It now aimed for total, national prohibition of the manufacture and sale of all intoxicating drinks. This caught the Prohibition Party off balance, as it did the WCTU, and both fell in, with lesser and greater eagerness, behind the Anti-Saloon League, which henceforth called itself the National Temperance Council.

The First World War caused much comprehensible hysteria. This was reflected in the official attitude toward drink in the English-speaking world, though not to my knowledge in France, Germany, Italy, or Russia. In England, King George V not only exchanged his and his relations' German surnames for English ones, but also proclaimed his extreme patriotism by announcing that he would not touch a drink until victory had been won. Perhaps a few courtiers followed his example: the soldiers who were to win that victory for him most certainly did not, as the quotation from Robert Graves on page 28 shows. More important was the effect upon the workers, usually referred to as the "munitions workers," who earned much overtime pay, though the ever-increasing manpower shortage brought about a great inflation of wages generally. As before, and again as today, the newly enriched proletariat spent its money in great measure on drink. The work in the factories suffered, not only from absenteeism (particularly on Mondays) but from the general lethargy and inefficiency that accompany hangover headaches and shaking hands.

The British Government passed its Defence of the Realm Act, which included the licensing hours of public houses. DORA was supposed to be repealed when George V took his first postwar drink, but the parts affecting the liquor trade at least are still with us. In Carlisle drunkenness was so bad that the pubs were nationalized. They are so still, and very unattractive places they are, too.

In the United States, although it remained neutral until 1917, boom conditions also prevailed, with much the same effects in the growing cities. It was as a war measure that the prohibitionists pushed through the Volstead Act (over President Wilson's veto, incidentally) and had the Eighteenth Amendment written into the Constitution. Even though the drys worked with great speed, while the searchlight of public interest was directed on the progress of the war, Prohibition did not come on the statute book until shortly after the war was over. It was not to be effective law until a year later, January 1920. This was to allow time for the saloonkeeper to sell his saloon, and the liquor merchant his stocks. It also gave the bootleggers plenty of time to get ready.

The supplementary volumes, published in 1922, to the eleventh edition of the *Encyclopaedia Britannica* contain a long article on Prohibition, which can have been part of United States law for only a year or so when the following conclusion was penned:

The most disinterested and intelligent observers, accustomed to judging public conditions and social facts, differed widely in their verdicts on prohibition, its economic results and general benefits or disadvantages to the public welfare in the first year of national prohibition. That is likely to be true for several years to come. The more authoritative opinion, however, seemed to be that the first effects had been generally beneficial; that the popular sentiment in support of effective prohibition was gaining in strength, and that the experiment would be continued and developed. The fears of lurking danger to social institutions or to the moral integrity of the people (which some critics believed to be inherent in prohibition), seemed likely to be outweighed by the economic and political advantages of freedom from the saloon, and the semblance, at least, of more orderly communities, less petty crime and less abject poverty. The majority of moderate drinkers seemed to be willing to sacrifice their personal liberty for these desirable results. The intemperate constitute a minority as compared with the total abstainers plus a majority of those who had been moderate users of intoxicating beverages, and their number may be expected to diminish from year to year. The business interests which were thought to be menaced by prohibition found, at the time when national and wartime prohibition went into effect, means of readjustment without great loss and without inflicting on the nation the burden of any scheme of compensation. The outlook for the future was in 1921 one of hope that new forces and new funds had now been released, which might be directed to providing normal recreation and facilities for social and community life which the saloon did not provide, but for which its very existence had precluded other provision being made.

Certainly the 1920s saw the upsurge of the ice-cream parlor and the drug store with its ice-cream counter as alternative meeting places, the billiard saloon and the bowling alley and, above all, the movies as places of entertainment. They did not, however, entirely replace the saloon, which was transformed into an illegal drinking center, now for all social classes, from such luxurious and world famous places as "21" (known to insiders by the names of its owners as "Jack and Charlie's") to the crummiest little back rooms with a peephole in the door. Since these were outside the law, the owners could get no help from the police in resisting the protection rackets of the gangsters, who now became a popular part of American folklore, the heirs of Jesse James and his like. But they were very different from those earlier outlaws.

The gangs rapidly organized the greater part of the speakeasy network which spread across the cities of the United States. They controlled the supply of liquor and they were gentle neither with the speakeasy proprietors nor with one another, a favorite weapon being the Thompson submachine gun, or tommy gun. Forced amalgamation of the gangs raised certain gangsters to great power. Al Capone was the most famous, and so clever was the secrecy of his Mafia methods that even he could be jailed only for income tax evasion. In Chicago above all, the Mafia (which now became and has remained an extremely powerful secret criminal organization in the United States) co-operated with the police. The rationale of this is obvious. It was far easier for the police to deal with one tightly controlled organization than with a great number of small gangs. In effect, the xenophobic Anti-Saloon League had substituted Sicilian gangsters for Irish or German barkeeps.

But the damage went far deeper than that. In the distant days before Prohibition the cops used to patrol beats on foot, and generally knew the inhabitants of their area. It would be wrong to say that they were popular, particularly in the working class districts, but then no police force ever is anywhere. But they were trusted, at least by the bourgeoisie.

An aunt of mine, living in one of the more expensive districts of Manhattan, met her local cop as she was going out of the front door on the very day that Prohibition became law. He respectfully touched his cap and said: "Excuse me, Mrs. —. I know you like to entertain. If ever you need anything to drink I can always get you a case of the real stuff."

She thanked him and henceforth used him as her bootlegger.

Not all the liquor sold by the bootlegger was "the real stuff," and some of it was positively noxious. Homemade moonshine was little better, since it was never allowed to mature. Many persons went blind. There are no statistics to compare the number of alcoholics before and after Prohibition (it was repealed in December 1933), but there can be little doubt that there must have been a great increase during Prohibition.

The big bootleggers smuggled the stuff in by the boatload,

principally to the innumerable inlets in the Florida coastline. Individual smugglers were usually less lucky. The customs officials ransacked suitcases with considerable roughness in their search for the odd bottle of scotch that the returned traveler might have concealed among his shirts. With the exception of the Russians, the American customs have remained the rudest, slowest, and roughest in the world. In fact Prohibition brought not only the law but also the law-enforcement officers into a disrepute from which they have never entirely recovered. True, they show little wish to be liked.

From the point of view of this book, more important perhaps is the general effect that Prohibition had on the drinking public, that is to say on the vast majority of Americans, by then of both sexes. The sense of sin was decreasing with the decline of religious fervor, but a residue of shame remained, particularly among heavy drinkers. To this was now added an element of secrecy which affected many with the knowledge that they were breaking not only God-made law (if they were several sorts of Christians) but also man-made law. The quick swig from the hip flask is not a healthy way to drink. Prohibition, in fact, laid for many drinkers the ground plan of alcoholism, for shame and secrecy are two of the hallmarks of that condition.

The Indians—I refer to the inhabitants of India—went one step further when they had obtained their independence of Britain in 1947. Total prohibition was imposed for religious reasons, with one exception. If a man or woman has a doctor's certificate stating that he is an alcoholic and therefore needs drink for medical reasons, he can buy what he wishes. The number of registered alcoholics in India is therefore phenomenally high. This also applies to anyone visiting that great country, who is advised to obtain some such certificate in his country of origin. What the statistical relationship is between real alcoholics and people who just wish for an occasional drink in India is therefore anybody's guess. Certainly this cannot make the problem of dealing with alcoholism in India any easier.

The human being is a very imperfect animal. As a close friend of mine, the late Dr. Sworn, used to say: "We are all failed apes." It is for this reason that we had to develop our brains so that we could invent tools, since we are neither swift nor strong. Furthermore, the human infant needs a quite prodigious length of time devoted to its care if it is to survive at all, and does not reach physical maturity for some fifteen to twenty years. Mental maturity comes even later, in some cases never.

Our brains did not cease to develop when we had invented tools, whether these be primitive ax-heads or space vehicles. Very early in our history we began to ask questions of an abstract nature: what are we and why do we behave as we do? The answer to the first was soon found. We are God's creation. (It may be that other animals have made the same discovery and that birdsong at dawn is in praise of the sun.) And our ancestors were, very early on, puzzled by death. Could so complex a being as a human living in an increasingly complex society simply disappear? Surely something must survive, and the very greatest men must be equipped to survive forever with all their trappings. The soul was invisible and immortal, destined to inhabit new human bodies, to receive back its own body in some great burial chamber, or to continue its bodiless existence elsewhere.

Human societies grew steadily more complicated, with wars and love and castes and religions and philosophies, and always this strange knowledge that no human being was perfect, that each was in some way or other a failure, that death was the destiny of us all. In some form or other our knowledge of death has always been ascribed to what Judaism and its successor religions have called "original sin." The clever failed ape had to pay a high price for his failure.

"Since recorded time," wrote Professor Moore in 1971, "man has used tranquilising agents to mitigate the harsh realities of life . . . whether these spring from physical discomfort . . . or mental stresses." The professor might have added that fantasy can be at least as harsh as reality. To give but two examples, there is unfounded sexual jealousy and there is the millionaire's fear of poverty because he has lost heavily on the stock exchange. Nor has the professor qualified his statement with the fact that some Red Indian tribes who knew not mescal used the ecstasy of the dance to exorcise "bad spirits," while the Maoris of what is now New Zealand seem to have had no form of sedative whatever before the arrival of the Europeans.

This whole book is about these "tranquilising agents," of which alcohol is the most common and the most traditional to Western men; it can be and frequently is abused as drunkenness, which can develop into alcoholism. Until very modern times there was no distinction between the two, and even now that line is blurred and ill-defined. All forms of abuse have always been regarded as wrong. *Nothing to excess,* such was Apollo's teaching and the more precious the gift of God or of the Gods, the greater the evil in its abuse through excess. So, too, and in almost exactly the same form was Confucius' message: no excess. The promiscuous lover, whether male or female, may amuse or occasionally titivate us, but we can hardly admire the private life of Catherine the Great or the Marquis de Sade, and most certainly not if we have any connection with them other than the printed page. The abuse of alcohol is similar and far more common than nymphomania or satyromania. *Gargantua* and *Pantagruel* may be great books, but they would surely have been hell to live through. And a real life Karamazov family should be shunned at all costs.

The alcoholic had been regarded, until very modern times, as an idiot, with proper assignment Bedlam; as a sinner; and as an anti-social menace, to be dealt with by the law. American Prohibition was the greatest, as it was the most futile, attempt to deal with drunkenness as a public menace by attempting to make alcohol disappear from the face of the land. (Indian prohibition is quite different: it was intended as a religious manifestation.) With the decline of religious authority in the West, what had been a case of sin became in larger measure a cause for shame. That is to say, drinking excessively became itself one of those causes of mental stress for which alcohol is the easiest palliative to hand. A downwards spiral is set up, which will be discussed later in this book. But on a more humane and sensible level the vacancy left by sin was filled by sickness, and the role of the priest or pastor inherited, briefly, by the psychoanalyst.

Alcoholism had been referred to as a disease by at least two English doctors in the late eighteenth century, though the use of the word alcoholism as meaning a disease is dated by the *Oxford English Dictionary* to 1852, which means that it had been used by two reputable writers at that time. It was not recognized as such, however, by the medical profession in Britain, America, and indeed virtually the entire world until very much later, while many doctors remain remarkably ignorant of this malady to this day. Dr. Dent, in Marty Mann's *Primer on Alcoholism*, is quoted in the appendix to the first edition (1952) as saying that he knew of only one hospital in Britain which allocated beds specifically for the treatment of alcoholism. In the postscript to the ninth British edition, Lord Forbes, writing apparently in 1974, says: "I can myself testify that it was impossible, in those early days, to get help from any London hospital for a chronically ill alcoholic. 'Take him away, he's drunk,' was the usual reaction of the admitting doctor. The only place in London we could get a sick alcoholic under cover was, curiously enough, Savile Row Police Station."

It was the same story in the United States, but far worse in the 1920s, when alcoholics were not only "drunks" but also breakers of the law. In New York the "Bowery bums" were untended alcoholics, a spectacle perhaps for sightseers. Obstreperous drunks were thrown into institutions little better if not worse than the Savile Row Police Station. And Alcoholics Anonymous was not founded until 1935.

Freud had invented psychoanalysis in 1910, shortly after his return to Vienna from America, and very soon the jargon of Freudianism became fashionable, particularly in America. In the 1920s psychoanalysts appeared in large numbers first in New York and later elsewhere. They were no more members of the medical profession than were osteopaths, and indeed had a similar, acerbic relationship with the doctors. But most of these analysts were prepared to handle rich alcoholics. Rich is here the operative word. The psychoanalysts maintained that unless their "patients" were compelled to pay exorbitant fees they would not appreciate, and therefore could not benefit from, psychoanalytical treatment. Since the money went into the analysts' own pockets, this is perhaps a good parallel to the alcoholic's "rationalizations" of which we shall be hearing later. Meanwhile, back in Vienna, Karl Kraus described psychoanalysis as a malady posing as its own cure.

It is not my intention here to summarize Freud's doctrines,

which made a very considerable contribution to the science of mental medicine, but rather to outline the simplified Freudianism of his epigones, which is not at all the same thing. Manes Sperber, Alfred Adler's close friend and biographer, has written that Freud performed a great service in that he "opened the bedroom door," which had been closed for far too long, but that he unfortunately "forgot that the bedroom is not the only room in the house."

Certainly popular Freudianism was interpreted as being based entirely on sex, specifically on the ill-named Oedipus complex, which was supposed to be universal. Ill-named, for the whole point of Sophocles' tragedies is that Oedipus did not know it was his father he had killed or that Jocasta was his mother: when he learned the horrors of his parricide and incest, he blinded himself. No story could be further from that of Freud, who as a very small boy had seen his mother remove her knickers in a train and had experienced a twinge of prepubertal curiosity which in his self-analysis (the model for all subsequent analysis) he interpreted as lust. Since most boys love their mothers, and girls their fathers, the Freudians hypothesized that everyone has an Oedipus or Electra complex. But since most of us would stoutly and truthfully deny having ever wished to kill or sleep with a parent, the Freudian unconscious (often misnamed the subconscious) had to be created in which to house primarily the Oedipus complex but also much else. An elaborate superstructure was built, breaking up the conscious into the id, basic animal desires; the ego, or personality of each individual; and the superego, or censor, which sternly controls the other two. By talking endlessly about himself or herself, using ideas in free association, the patient can allow the analyst to penetrate through the superego and the ego to the id (which is not very interesting) and even more so to the unconscious (which *is* interesting, for it is there that according to the unprovable assertions of the Freudians the "real" truth is to be found).

Inhibitions are created by the superego and, to a lesser extent, by the ego. The sedative effect of alcohol weakens or destroys inhibitions. (Sleep has a similar effect.) The alcoholic drinks, very often, precisely to achieve this state: the Freudians maintained

that his superego was intolerable, and that if he could be taught
the truth (which lay in his Oedipus complex and the rest of his
unconscious) he would be freed of the need to drink.

In other terms, the Oedipus complex filled the gap left by the
religious concept of original sin as science replaced religion,
Marxism replaced social charity and responsibility, and so on.

Therefore, when the doctors, most of whom knew nothing
whatsoever about alcoholism even though a rather high proportion were and are alcoholics themselves, rebuffed their alcoholic
patients, ascribing their alcoholism usually to mere weakness of
will, those patients who could afford to do so not infrequently
turned to the psychoanalysts. The treatment often lasted for
years, and undoubtedly there were cases where the analyst was
able to help in some other field by allowing his patient to "talk it
out" in the free association of ideas, which it was believed gradually gave a picture of the unconscious in terms that the conscious
mind could understand. And in some of these happy cases, the
disturbed person may have drunk excessively because of his disturbance. Thus could the analyst claim a measure of success in
curing alcoholism. What he had in fact very occasionally cured
was some other problem, almost certainly of a sexual nature.
With the disappearance of this problem there often went the
desire to drink excessively, though that problem may have made
itself most obvious in the sufferer's drinking habits and indeed
found expression and therefore as much relief *in vino veritas* as
on the psychoanalyst's couch.

To that extent, and to that extent only, can psychoanalysis be
claimed as a cure for alcoholism. In the vast majority of cases it
was, and is, a total failure, for alcoholism is not a manifestation
of the Freudian Oedipus complex, from which, in any event,
only a minute number of people suffer.

Far less important in the social scene, but perhaps far more so
in our search for truth, was Alfred Adler's substitute for original
sin. Adler was a contemporary of Freud's, originally a friend but
later, as was the case with almost all Freud's friends, an adver-
sary, even an enemy. While accepting, with rather different emphasis, the basic concepts of the unconscious, id, ego, and
superego, he did not go along with the Oedipus business, and his

prime motive in his analysis of human disturbance was the inferiority feeling (for which he also claimed universal application). The German for this is *Minderwertigkeitsgefuehl,* and it is usually mistranslated as "inferiority complex," no doubt to match Freud's invention. This is totally incorrect, for what Adler wrote about was not a complex at all. This feeling of inferiority derives from our long period of helplessness after birth, our protracted reliance on others first for mere survival and then for the vast human paraphernalia known, briefly, as education that enables us to become adult members of our society. It varies greatly in intensity and also in manifestation. For example, some of us have never felt particularly shy, even in adolescence, while a surprisingly high proportion of adolescents actually commit suicide. Boys will usually react against their fathers and teachers, and girls against their mother and accepted modes of behavior, at some point around or after puberty. This reaction may be mild or extremely violent, but it has nothing whatever to do with Oedipus. None of us will ever outgrow this feeling of inferiority to somebody or something. In generalized terms it manifests itself in the so-called generation gap, which seems to take each adult generation by surprise as it sees its offspring determined to remodel society, science, art, the universe itself. As Molière put it sarcastically in the mouth of a young man: *"Nous avons changé tout cela."* It can, as it were, work sideways, as we have seen in much of the feminist movement. It can find compensation in bullying, even in brutality, in the determination to prove, honorably or dishonorably, that one is not inferior to one's fellows. It can seek reassurance in collectivity, the collective strength of the artistic "group," of the political party, of the nation, which in turn can express itself in the overcoming of other groups or parties or nations—in a word, in the momentary glory of victory. It can thus be both very productive and horribly destructive. It will find its happiest release in love, love of husband or wife, love of children, love of God.

In alcoholic terms a couple of drinks, particularly if taken with protective friends, will dim the inhibitions that the inferiority feeling creates. More, however, may bring it back in one of its nastier self-defense manifestations, in self-pity, boasting, or even fighting. And it is directly connected with the alcoholic's periods of shame.

The third great psychologist of that generation was the Swiss Carl Gustav Jung. In the opinion of this writer Jung created a view of the world which is an aesthetic triumph comparable, perhaps, to that of Goethe or even Dante, lacking the poetry. He was, in effect, a great artist. Jung was also a scientist and a teacher, who teaches us to understand our own actions and attitudes and those of others far better than does Freud. Freud probably cast the longer shadow, but then, like Marx, he stood against the sunrise.

CHAPTER XIV

What Is It?

The World Health Organization has defined the alcoholic as follows: "Alcoholics are those excessive drinkers whose dependence upon alcohol has attained such a degree that it shows a noticeable mental disturbance or an interference with their bodily or mental health, their interpersonal relationships and their smooth social and economic functioning, or shows the prodromal signs of such development."

Prodromal means the approaching signs of a disease. Translated into clearer English, this means that you can be an alcoholic before you know it. Some theoreticians go further than this and assert that an alcoholic is an alcoholic from birth and remains so until his death, *even though he may never take a drink in his life*. This would mean that alcoholism is a hereditary disease, and also that the reason so many young people "take the pledge" and keep it is either because of a built-in-defense mechanism or because of the example given them by drunken parents or grandparents. This last explanation is, however, directly contrary to the Mendelian theory of heredity, by which we are living according to genes that existed in our forebears at any point between now and the mid-eighteenth century.

Mrs. Mann, in her *Primer on Alcoholism,* gives a far simpler definition: "An alcoholic is someone whose drinking causes a continuing problem in any department of his life."

The World Health Organization also calls potable alcohol (ethyl alcohol) a potential drug of dependence. In this it is comparable to the "hard" drugs, the opiates, morphines, and hallucinogens, such as laudanum, heroin, and LSD. However, only in the case of the alcoholic does it do such harm as the hard drug, and alcoholics are fairly rare. The WHO estimates that of those who drink only 5 to 6 per cent become alcoholics. In earlier pages I have given the figure of 6 to 7 per cent. This, too, is now generally believed to be too low, since most alcoholics will not admit to, or will try to conceal, their condition, and a proportion must succeed. Let us therefore pick on a quite arbitrary figure, 10 per cent.

Professor Jellinek, the most famous founding father of the modern study of alcoholism, broke down alcoholism into five main types:

The Alpha Alcoholic is a psychological case. He drinks reactively, to find relief from pain both mental and physical, reactive depression, anger, and so on. But primarily he drinks from endogenous depression, which is inbuilt, without apparent cause, and may be hereditary. This feeling of *angst,* in which motiveless fear plays an important part, can be acute.

The Beta Alcoholic drinks because of his environment, physical and social. He may drink to dispel the misery of living in a slum, the boredom of life on an Indian reservation or, for women, of endless, repetitive housework; or he and she may drink because they move in a society where much drinking is normal behavior. Either riches or poverty can thus be a contributory cause, but with poverty the economic effects of drinking become immediately apparent. As will be seen, writers, painters, and musicians will often drink when not working, using alcohol as a mild relief from banality. According to the behaviorists, and in particular the Marxists, since environment is the cause of everything, it must also be the cause of drink.

The Gamma Alcoholic has a peculiar form of allergy to drink. He or she will take one drink and will immediately be overcome with a raging thirst for more. This type will then, according to capacity, drink at great speed, say a bottle in an hour, until he or she passes out, suffering meanwhile an almost complete personality change. Red Indians, or those with Red Indian blood, seem to be particularly susceptible to this type of alcoholism, which often culminates in suicide (see Appendix V). It is described in Edgar Allan Poe's suicidal poem *For Annie*, from which I quote two verses:

> And oh! of all tortures
> That torture the worst
> Has abated—the terrible
> Torture of thirst
> For the naphthaline river
> Of Passion accurst:
> I have drunk of a water
> That quenches all thirst!

The Delta Alcoholic is the individual who cannot abstain, who must always have a glass in his hand. He may be completely sodden, but he is seldom drunk. He may indeed function brilliantly and for a very long time, provided his physique does not collapse. Winston Churchill and F. E. Smith (the first Lord Birkenhead) may have been delta alcoholics. So presumably were Alexander the Great and innumerable men of commerce, the arts, and the professions.

The Epsilon Alcoholic goes on occasional drinking bouts of two or three days, between which he will be sober. In some cultures this will be almost normal weekend behavior. But the intervals between the bouts will tend to become shorter. The liver, which is usually the organ to suffer the most immediate damage from alcohol, has almost fantastic powers of recuperation. Given a rest from Monday to Friday, it will usually recover; between Tuesday and Thursday it will not. Since the native Irish and Scots are very heavy weekend drinkers but are usually sober or teetotal on weekdays, the incidence of cirrhosis of the liver is low. However, a series of weddings or funerals in a series of midweeks may soon be too much even for the most docile Irish liver. Unless under some form of calendar control, the epsilon alcoholic can approximate to the gamma.

There remain, at present, the two great unknowns about alcoholism. Why should so small a number of drinkers become alcoholics, perhaps one in ten? The whole of scientific thought, at

least until very recent times, was predicated upon the somewhat
naïve and simplistic formula that B always follows A, until Z is
reached, at which point the subject is finished, closed, completely understood. Hence the apparent antithesis with religion.
Not all the greatest scientists have denied the existence of the supernatural. (Newton is perhaps the most obvious case, though it
is presumptuous to assume—as it has been assumed—that Gal-
ileo was being hypocritical when he accepted the wisdom of the
priesthood as greater than his own, in his own field, while Pavlov
insisted, in the teeth of Bolshevik tyranny, that his "conditioned
reflex" theories applied to dogs, not to humans.) And in the most
scientific of the sciences, in mathematics itself, the quantum
theory has long played ducks and drakes with the cause-and-
effect rigidity of eighteenth- and nineteenth-century scientific
thought. Meanwhile those much overestimated "humanist" brains
of the Enlightenment, overestimated that is when not engaged
upon purely practical matters, had done their best to discredit
religious thought, not without considerable effect, while the B-
follows-A simplification continues to plague, not always unhap-
pily, the popular forms of scientific or pseudoscientific thought.

Alcoholism is a psychosomatic malady. The nineteenth century
rather impertinently abused the Greek word psyche to mean
mind, not, as it does in Greek, spirit. But the mind, being housed
within a tangible "thing," the nervous system and especially the
brain, is more acceptable to the materialistic thinker, who has his
own body or soma. Psychosomatic thus refers both to the body
and to the mind as a product, or even a part, of that body. The
attempt to give the unconscious a major role in the functions of
the mind was in reality an attempt to reincarnate, in the literal
meaning of that verb, what had been a *sine qua nihil* of religious
experience. Nevertheless, psychosomatic was a conveniently
minted word, if a semantically inexact one.

Similarly the genes, as the mechanical transmitters of heredity,
are scientifically convenient. Nobody seems to have noted that
the sixty-four ancestors who form the base line of Mendel's inverted triangle correspond exactly to the sixty-four quarterings
needed to achieve complete medieval nobility. But perhaps this
is as coincidental as the sixty-four squares on the chessboard.

Similarly, again, when we read and talk of environment we are talking about the world in the old ritualistic sense of "the world, the flesh and the devil." What, by the way, has happened to the devil? The scientists seem to have mislaid him, and the Christian churches have forgotten him. The poets have not, and perhaps his fingerprints are to be detected on Jung's shadow persona. Certainly he would appear to be very much in evidence in certain aspects of alcoholism.

What then is the cause of alcoholism among a small proportion of those who drink? Professor Moore does not attempt to give a B-follows-A explanation, but plunges far deeper into the scientific alphabet. "In the life of each individual who misuses alcohol," he says, "factors from all of the three following sources—his psyche and soma, his environment, and his genes—contribute to the end result."

I myself would bet quite heavily on his genes, but what precisely do they pass on to him? Does he inherit alcoholism? If so, the number of alcoholics would surely be very much greater than it is, while it is the non-alcoholics who would be flukes, 10, 5, or 3 per cent. Does he inherit addiction? This would seem far more probable, since almost all of us are addicted to something, be it tobacco, coffee, tea, some special form of food, work, music, or collecting stamps. Is it endogenous depression, which can (but by no means always does) find relief in sedatives, the quickest and most obtainable of which is alcohol?

The scientists have not yet answered that question, and Professor Moore is surely wise to keep his options open.

Again why do a proportion—truly a much higher proportion— of prodromal status alcoholics slip over the border, at no predetermined point, into the true diease? The professor says: "Once the constitutional barrier has broken down, the individual is in the grip of a progressive disease over which he has a swiftly declining control." He is in effect then headed for Skid Row, and fast, but again only 2 per cent of diseased alcoholics reach what is perhaps more accurately defined as the Korsakoff condition, when the human being becomes a sort of vegetable, a living organism without a mind or a memory, interested solely in obtaining drink. Death will usually, reform sometimes, have saved him from this protracted but apparently not very unhappy ending.

We do not know what is the constitutional change that leads directly to the diseased condition. We may be able to heat hydrogen to a level twice that of the sun's center, but our microscopes cannot detect what is apparently the appearance—or maybe the disappearance—of a biochemical agent that would account for this constitutional change. Does it exist? The biochemist who isolates it should surely be given the Nobel Prize for Medicine. To judge by the precedents of leprosy, smallpox, tuberculosis, and other diseases, once the disease is understood it should be curable.

At present it is incurable and progressive.

CHAPTER XV

Drunk's Progress: Childhood

If we are to accept *in toto* the theory of hereditary alcoholism, an infant is a drunkard before it is born, indeed potentially so before it is conceived. However, the most we can say for sure is that a problem drinker's child may not be born at all. A drunkard, usually the child's father, may inflict such physical damage on its pregnant mother as to bring about a miscarriage. He may of course not be himself an alcoholic, but merely a psychopath. Let us assume that he is an alcoholic. In extreme cases the "personality change" which will be discussed below can turn a normally stable man, including normally sane alcoholics, into temporary psychopaths. On the other hand, the damage on the pregnant woman may not be inflicted deliberately. He may stumble and knock her over, he may cause some heavy object to fall on her, he may involve her in many forms of accident, the most common being the car accident (see Appendix II). In which case he (or she, if she is the alcoholic) may run into another car carrying a pregnant woman, a person quite unknown to the drunken driver, and cause her to miscarry or even kill her.

It has been reckoned in the past that there is one woman alcoholic for every three male addicts. Like most statistics concerning this subject, the figure is neither well established nor immutable. There seems, on the face of it, no reason why there should not be parity between the sexes. Hitherto it has been far more shameful for a woman to be drunk than for a man. This, however, is rapidly on the decrease, one of militant feminism's more curious triumphs.

"Old Charlie was pretty far gone last night, wasn't he?"

Old Charlie's friends will usually say this without any special condemnation, indeed perhaps even with a chuckle, unless

Charlie has been offensive, verbally or even physically, to one or more of them. In France it used to be said that a man had to have had gonorrhea at least three times before he could apply for a tobacconist's license. In the English-speaking world a middle-aged man will feel no shame in admitting to a dose of clap when young. With women it is utterly different, and this also applies to drunkenness. Even women who themselves drink heavily will say: "I thought Mary was quite disgusting last night. If there is one thing I cannot stand, it is the sight of a drunken woman."

And if Mary is pregnant, her drunkenness is not only disgusting but well-nigh criminal. A pregnant woman's drunkenness can have a physical, and possibly a psychological, effect upon the embryo, though not necessarily (but see Appendix IV). However, a drunken woman can quite easily fall down a flight of stairs and miscarry, particularly in the third month. She can also usually drive a car, though will be less likely to do so than the man she is with. But once again the potential alcoholic she is carrying may never see the light of day.

For these reasons women have, until and including the present time, tended to drink in secret. For this they have also rather more opportunity than men. They may be alone in the house all day, and they do the shopping. Until quite recently they did not go into bars or city pubs alone, unless they were prostitutes. They would hesitate even to buy a bottle of anything stronger than sherry from an off-license, particularly if they were secret drinkers, for the purchase of a bottle of whiskey might betray their secret. Nowadays, when so much household shopping is done in supermarkets, a woman can quite easily put a bottle of spirits in her basket along with the detergent and the vegetables and all the rest of it. Yet even so the secret drinker may be afraid of being seen by a friend.

Another way the unborn alcoholic may be disposed of is by abortion, which is now legal in Britain and America and will probably be so soon in the rest of the Western world. But this is recent. In the last century, and well into this, one of the nicknames given to gin was "mother's ruin." This did not mean that gin could ruin the mother of a growing family—though of course it could—but rather that the rapid drinking of a bottle of gin when immersed in a very hot bath, during the critical third month, would save a pregnant girl from having to find an illegal abortionist, who was likely to be either expensive or dangerous or both. In my autobiography, *Through the Minefield,* I described how, in 1937, at the age of eighteen, I attempted to procure an abortion for a girl of my own age. I failed. Nor did the "mother's ruin" technique apparently succeed, though it may have. We were both drinking heavily, almost desperately, and the child, which was born two months prematurely, lived for only a few hours.

Once a child is born, it can be started on a career of addiction at a very early age. I have heard of, but never seen, women tranquilize a crying child by putting beer, or in France wine, in its bottle. I have read of an American who, after having tranquilized her baby with whiskey, took it to the doctor, who diagnosed: "Madam, your baby is suffering from the DTs."

In India, in the days of the British Raj, the famous amahs who nursed the Englishwomen's babies are said not infrequently to have calmed their little charges with a touch of opium in the milk. But these must all be very exceptional cases.

The question then arises about drinking in childhood and adolescence. Can a child be *taught* to drink sensibly and in moderation? In a household of total absteemers, of Plymouth Brethren, say, the question simply does not arise. But the reaction can be fearful. A man who knows the Arabs well has informed me that, of ten Arabs he knew intimately and who drank, nine were alcoholics. If these figures are correct, they represent far more than the 10 per cent or less of the "normal" drinking population who contract the disease at some point in their lives. Of course there are other factors involved. An individual brought up in a faith which he or she later abandons has lost far more than his abstentionist convictions. To deprive a man or woman of faith in God which, under whatsoever form and with whatsoever sense of good or evil, the individual has previously worshiped, is not necessarily to deprive that person of all sense of proportion: hence the large number of lapsed Baptists and Mormons who do *not* become alcoholics or, indeed, sinners against society in any form. On the other hand, it does render self-control infinitely more

difficult, for it makes the individual dependent solely on his own
willpower and on social convention, without the aid of that su-
preme authority to which he or she has been accustomed.

Whether this has the same effect on an entire society is an almost unanswerable question. In Europe it seems that it does. European history, and in this we must include America, has seen in
the last few centuries a repeated falling off in religious belief
punctuated and temporarily reversed by very strong religious
reformations or revivals. But so many other factors are involved,
such as national wealth and national well-being, that it is impossible to ascribe national drinking habits to the strength or weakness of religious belief. Furthermore, we lack the statistics to
compare the amount that was drunk in, say, Wales immediately
before and after the Wesleyan revival. We do know that Father
Matthew's Irish temperance crusade of 1838 and the immediate
succeeding years persuaded some four million Irishmen and
women, or half the population of the time, to take the pledge.
We also know that all this was forgotten in the Famine of 1845–
50 and that it was not until 1889 that the Jesuits in Ireland organized another, rather less successful but more durable, campaign
of total abstinence, the Pioneers. Perhaps this has endured so
successfully, with two thousand branches and a strength of
several hundred thousand, precisely because the Pioneers are not
anonymous, but wear a badge visible to all. They are therefore
respected, and few Irishmen will offer a grown Pioneer a drink.
On the other hand, when the boy or girl is forcibly enrolled at
the time of his or her first Communion, the badge will often be
quite rapidly removed from the blouse or the lapel. This does not
mean either that the ex-Pioneer will cease going to church or
that he will become an alcoholic.

Only the conclusion is certain. The abstainer who never takes
a drink in his or her life can obviously never become an alcoholic. It seems almost, but not quite, equally certain that the person who has abstained for religious reasons (and apart from
physical health, a loathing of the taste, and extreme poverty there
are really no others) and who begins to drink is more likely to
become an alcoholic than the person who has drunk normally all
his or her drinking life.

The position of the convert, that is to say the grown man or woman who has accepted a religious belief, be this Roman Catholicism or another faith, in place of atheism, agnosticism, or the faith of his or her childhood, is rather different and is dependent on the personality of the convert. Many are of the "all or nothing" sort, who are attracted by the dramatic force of religious experience. The extremism of many converts is well known. Should such a one lapse, should the pendulum in effect swing the other way, a lapsed extremism is likely to ensue, and one symptom of this may be a determination to sin, as defined by the abandoned religion. Such a person has no interest in temperance, as truly defined. If his or her former faith forbade drinking, the man or woman will probably become a heavy drinker and very possibly an alcoholic. But it must be repeated that this depends very much on the personality of the individual and not upon the nature of the religion.

But when should the normal drinking life start? The Latin nations give wine to quite small children, the French in particular. True, it is usually diluted with water and even that is not given in very large quantities. But from the age of about six or seven most French children are given a little wine once or even twice a day. Only very recently have the French schools, when sending their children on outings, ceased packing wine with the sandwiches. And it used to be argued that as a result of this early training fewer Frenchmen became drunkards than Englishmen or Germans. Certainly, at least until very recently, one saw far fewer drunkards on the streets of Paris than on those of Berlin or London or New York, while in higher social strata drunken Frenchmen at, say, the end of a dinner party were very rare indeed, drunken Frenchwomen virtually unknown. But the French soaked steadily. Often in Parisian bistros, at 6 or 7 A.M., have I seen workmen downing a glass or two of cheap *rouge* before setting off to work. These men were not drunkards, equivalent to the American or Englishman who has his eye-opener to recover from last night's excessive drinking. These were perfectly normal French workingmen, behaving as they had behaved and would continue to behave all their lives. Yet, as can be seen in Appendix III, the French have a higher intake of alcohol than any other nation listed. (However, the Iron Curtain countries' figures are certainly worthless, and it is probable that the Russians, Poles, and Hungarians drink more.) This does not necessarily mean that there are more alcoholics in France than elsewhere, but it would at least indicate that this is a probability. Certainly General de Gaulle was deeply concerned with alcoholism in France, which in his day caused greater damage to the French economy than the total gain brought by the wine and spirits industry, an industry which in all its aspects, from the vineyard to the wine waiter, employs approximately one third of the French working population. (See Appendix I for another estimate of the damage to industry by alcoholism.) An attempt to curb drinking by Prime Minister Mendès-France in the 1950s was a failure. It is probable that more Frenchmen are *intoxiqués,* that is to say suffer from a toxic condition, than any other Western nation.

What is a certainty is that proportionately more Frenchmen die of cirrhosis of the liver than the inhabitants of any other country for which we have reliable statistics. Cirrhosis of the liver is not limited to drunkards, and the rich heaviness of much French food, as eaten by the middle classes, while being the best in the world to eat, is a minor contributory factor. Nor do all drunkards have bad livers. Dylan Thomas's autopsy showed that his liver was in apple-pie order. But there is a connection between the two. And unlike the Irishman, the Frenchman seldom gives his liver a holiday. I recall walking down what must have been the medical street of Bordeaux. In France doctors are permitted by law to hang out their shingles, and in almost every house there was one who specialized in *maux de foie.*

Jews, both in Israel and the Diaspora, also give their children wine, but in a very different way. In an Orthodox Jewish household the main meal of Friday and of the Sabbath is a religious ritual (this lingers on among Christians as the Mass or Holy Communion) and part of the ritual is a very small amount of wine. It is not, in effect, "a drink," and as will be seen in Appendix III, Israel is at the very bottom of the table for alcoholic consumption.

I have a great many Jewish friends, both Orthodox and not, and in my experience most of them drink with great moderation, while those who drink to excess are very bad drinkers indeed.

When I asked one Jewish friend why he drank so little, he said
that he hated drunkenness: born in eastern Poland, he was old
enough to identify intoxication with the drunken Cossacks of his
childhood and later, in Berlin, with the drunken Nazi S.A. Another told me, quite simply, that he hated becoming befuddled
and losing his wits, or seeing his friends lose theirs. I have one
very clever Jewish friend who has alternated between long bouts
of extreme drunkenness, so that one thought he must surely sink
into the deepest and most irremediable forms of alcoholism, and
longer periods of light drinking and complete sobriety. He was
born and brought up in Budapest. Perhaps it was the Hungarian
who got drunk; the Jew who remained sober.

The English-speaking and Germanic peoples have a different
attitude toward drinking among the young. Here a certain economic class distinction is in evidence, though in all classes it is
regarded as bad for children to drink. In general, bars, public
houses, beer halls, and so on have a minimum age for customers
—usually about eighteen—below which it is illegal to sell them
drinks, though this varies from country to country, from time to
time, and in America from state to state. However, it may be
said, roughly, to correspond with legal coming of age, the right
to vote, to join the armed forces and so on. This seems quite logical. But it does not in practice work out quite like this. Children
used to start to drink at the time when they got their first job, for
in the working class before then they had no money with which
to buy the stuff. The last twenty years, however, have seen a vast
increase in the prosperity of the young, mostly as a result of
higher wages. This has not had altogether happy results, in that
it has led to a great increase in vandalism and, in England particularly, to "soccer hooliganism," the wrecking of trains and indeed juvenile crime generally. In England, also, this has led to
race riots on a minor scale, usually between the white English
and colored immigrants. Paki-bashing, which means the beating
up of Pakistanis, had almost become a recognized juvenile sport
a dozen or so years ago. And the children of immigrants, born in
Britain and therefore more self-assured, have in some cases re-
sponded in kind. Most of this juvenile crime is committed under
the influence of drink. Although the publicans in general refuse

to serve the very young, age is difficult to detect. Furthermore, anyone over the age of fifteen, or at least looking fifteen, can buy liquor in the many new supermarkets. And these juvenile delinquents pose a severe problem to the law enforcement authorities. They cannot, indeed probably should not, be sent to prison at an age so formative that it will tend to turn them into permanent criminals. Nor are the reform schools (known in England as Borstals) adequate either in space or in techniques for "reforming" these young people. Magistrates in any event tend to be very lenient toward them. In Ireland a housebreaker of sixteen is usually remanded, to be on good behavior for three or six months. And from this great number of drunken hooligans and childish criminals must come many of the alcoholics of the future. It is a very serious problem.

It is made the more so in that increased female emancipation has led to more and more young girls copying their boy friends and drinking with them. It is even more difficult to tell the difference between a made-up girl of sixteen and one of eighteen than it is with a boy. The publican who is not too squeamish about serving children can often say, quite honestly, that he thought a girl was of age when she was not. In America the "blackboard jungle" type of school is a sure breeding ground of hooligans, usually drunken, sometimes drugged. Nowhere can the police cope fully with this plethora of petty crime by the very young. Massive unemployment, though cushioned by welfare, has one frequent result among the young, who are particularly susceptible to an absence of jobs when they leave school. They have nothing to do, but they have money in their pockets. In many cases this will be spent on drink. It does not augur well for the future.

The story among the bourgeoisie is rather different. They, both boys and girls, will usually stay at school longer and will generally go straight from school to college. They will thus not be thrown out into the world, and onto the labor market, until they are about twenty-one or twenty-two years old. Any tendency toward hooliganism is kept in check with comparative ease. Drunkenness, too, is among middle-class schoolboys and schoolgirls rather rare, while addiction to dope—which sprang up rather suddenly and assumed almost epidemic proportions in the 1960s—seems to be on the wane among the young throughout the Western world, although this may be premature optimism. Cannabis, or pot, is still smoked in large quantities and has become almost an accepted ingredient of society. It is usually a substitute for alcohol, in that it, too, is a sedative. It is said to be non-addictive and is probably therefore less dangerous than alcohol. In the very limited experience of this writer it is an unsatisfactory substitute, producing the sedative effects and nothing more. People smoking pot become very slow in their conversation and in their reactions. They do not appear to be much of a danger to anybody, except when behind the wheel of a car, where quick reactions are often essential if an accident is to be avoided. The hallucinogens, of which LSD is the most popular, are far more dangerous, being both habit-forming and capable quite rapidly of producing schizophrenia, psychotic illness, and sometimes permanent brain damage. It is this type of drug, together with cocaine and heroin, which seems to be on the wane among the young.

The drinking habits among the adolescent bourgeois have changed little in the past few generations. At boarding schools boys were not allowed to drink at all. Now the older ones are allowed a little beer. Those who attended day schools were not usually allowed to drink at home. The general exception was Christmas, when a glass or so of wine was permitted, sometimes more. And at parties the adolescent usually managed to sneak a drink or two, particularly the boys. The girls seemed to be, and probably were, less interested.

It was at college or university that legal drinking began, though here too there were restrictions. When I went up to Oxford in 1938, all pubs, bars, and other places designed solely for public liquor consumption were barred. To be caught in one by the proctor or by his runners ("bulldogs") was a punishable offense which, if sufficiently repeated and detected, meant being sent down, or dismissed from the university. On the other hand, we were allowed to order what we wished, either from the college buttery or from the wine merchants who were usually only too anxious to give credit, since if the undergraduate could not pay his debts his parents almost invariably would. Beer was served in Hall with dinner, and we were allowed to dine in restaurants and there order whatever we desired. We also had clubs, where we drank, often heavily. I understand that little has changed since then, save that pubs are no longer off limits—this is probably a socially egalitarian measure—and the wine merchants are less anxious to extend credit.

It used to be said that one of the reasons a boy went to a university was that he should there learn how to drink. This did not mean learn how to get drunk. Quite the contrary. A drunk is a bore, and though the older generation may tell the younger this *ad nauseam,* they will seldom be listened to. But when a young man's contemporaries avoid him, or walk away, because he is a drunken bore, the impact will be immediate and usually salutary. He will either drink decently or perhaps sometimes not at all, but should emerge into the world capable of drinking socially and not to excess.

Many of those, of course, who get drunk choose the company of others with the same inclination. From these little cliques there undoubtedly spring many middle-class alcoholics, though far from all their members go that way. Of my Oxford friends, almost all of whom drank to excess, some are alcoholics, more are dead, while the remainder have either become teetotalers for health reasons or have remained heavy drinkers. However, they were not my friends solely as drinking companions. They were also, and not incidentally, high among the more intelligent and artistically inclined of my contemporaries. This is not surprising. Such people tend to be sensitive and are therefore more attracted to, sometimes more in need of, the sedative qualities of alcohol.

A very few of the then limited number of girl undergraduates drank with us. What has happened to them I do not know.

I believe that much the same circumstances prevailed and still prevail in American colleges, in particular the Ivy League ones, which are so closely modeled on Oxford and Cambridge. And also at similar schools of higher education, such as schools of art and music.

CHAPTER XVI

Prodromal Phase?

I now return to my own case history, which I broke off at Chapter I. By the time I went to Bermuda, in March 1946, I was a discharged, reserve major in the Army of the United States, having regained my American citizenship, which I had sacrificed when I first joined the British Army, and I was twenty-six years old. I had been married for the second time for two years, and was in fact in every way a grown man. At least as important, apart from a few months as a schoolmaster at a somewhat farcical school in Bermuda I never again took any sort of a job, for I was determined henceforth to be my own master, even to the extent of putting up with considerable, at times almost desperate, poverty. I must have done quite well in the Army, for they wished me to stay on, with the rank of lieutenant colonel, or to be a founder member of the Central Intelligence Agency, the CIA, but both these offers I declined. I valued my freedom above all else, and I wanted to write at last.

I was able to go to Bermuda for two reasons. I had three months' accumulated leave on full pay, and an aunt of mine had a cottage there which she said I might have rent free. It was when my pay ran out that I got the job as a schoolmaster, for I a cottage there which she said I might have rent free. It was able to complete during the long summer holidays that began almost as soon as I took the job.

Bermuda, at first, was bliss. The military, and most of the naval, forces had gone. The tourists had not begun to return. There were still no cars. All was sea, sun, and sand. And there was unlimited food and drink. After half-starved, half-parched,

filthy, rationed, wartime Europe, Bermuda in 1946 was glorious.
Furthermore, my family had been intimately connected with the
island for more than half a century—my grandfather had owned
a house there—and when money began to run low, my credit
was even better than it had been at Oxford. My wife and I ordered Bacardi rum by the case, and drank it with Coca-Cola or
fresh lime juice. I was happy as a sandboy, writing, swimming,
going a dark brown in color, drinking cuba libres beneath a par-
asol, reading, in fact leading a life the exact contrary of the one I
had led for some six years. Bermudan society was rather dull,
but we soon gave up going to their Dolmetch-type cocktail parties. Everybody assumed I was very rich, but then almost everyone has, everywhere, because I have always lived that way,
whether I have had any money or not. Usually, as a matter of
fact, I have not.

This seems a good point at which to speak of my morals, both
sexual and financial, simply because they are relevant to my
story of drinking. In my youth, as the reader will have gathered,
I had many affairs, of shorter or longer duration. I, or my happy-
go-lucky manner, or more probably both, must have appealed to
the girls, for when I asked them to go to bed with me they usually agreed. I did not normally regard this as constituting any
sort of contract, but rather as an exchange of pleasures. The
feminist movement has nothing to teach me, since I have always
regarded women as my own sex's equals. On the other hand,
when in love with a girl I have usually not wanted any other,
and have assumed a reciprocal loyalty, if that be the word. This
is why I was so hideously depressed when I was at Camp Ritchie
and my wife wrote me that she was being unfaithful. Nor was
my jealousy relieved by reciprocation in kind. I have remained
jealous ever since, though often this has been that alcoholic
jealousy, a beastly fantasy, already referred to. But my sexual
morality has basically been limited to not stealing my friends'
wives or girl friends, even when the girl has hinted that she was
not averse. I knew too much about jealousy to risk hurting my
friends.

My financial morals have been, from the Calvinist point of
view, equally deplorable. While always paying my debts to

small tradesmen, and repaying money borrowed from friends, I am in no way worried by the fact that thirty years later I still owe money to certain millionaire Bermudan wine merchants or, come to that, to exorbitantly expensive Oxford tailors who had no business giving such credit to undergraduates in the first place, and who priced their goods on the assumption that a small percentage of their customers would never pay. I have, on the other hand, never written a rubber check, or sponged on friends, but have lent money to people in need, and been delighted when such loans were repaid. I have always regarded Polonius's advice on this subject as being as foolish as Shakespeare doubtless intended it to be.

All this is relevant because in my drinking days—at least until very near their end—I felt neither guilt nor shame, and feel none in retrospect. Nor would I be able to write this book honestly if I did. I was not a "secret bottle" man. I drank because I liked both the taste and the effect, indeed I drank much as I made love. So far as I was concerned, the bottle did not need to be "liberated." When people told me, as long ago as Bermuda, that I drank too much, I would reply that if and when drinking interfered with my work, my private life, my friendships or my health, then would be time for me to consider cutting down. In the end it was my health that collapsed, but only some thirty years after my arrival in Bermuda.

Not that I remained in Bermuda all that time. Two and a half years was too long, and for the last six months I was suffering depression, reactive depression, I think, because I was caught in a dilemma: I could no longer afford to go on living in Bermuda and I could not afford to go anywhere else.

I had written two novels, but had gotten stuck halfway through a third. (When eventually I finished it, several years later, it turned out to be my worst: this has taught me never to go back to unfinished work, for one's mood cannot be the same.) I mooned about in a Bermuda, to which the tourists had returned, with an increase in prices and the introduction of cars. Nor could I drink in cheap pubs, for these were, in practice, reserved to the blacks, who were barred from the expensive white men's bars. I had never lived anywhere else where a color bar existed, and I found it curiously humiliating that I could not, by law, establish easy contact with a large segment of the population. When I invited a black photographer to my cottage, I was reprimanded by my Bermudan acquaintances. Of course I took no notice of this, and invited the black editor of a local paper, for which my wife wrote a sort of gossip column. It was not really a success, and they never invited us back. After two years, I was beginning to dislike Bermuda, and I was glad when my mother gave me enough money to get away.

I went to New York to look for a job. I did not look very hard. I was starved for conversation, and I spent most of my time talking to other writers in bars I could not afford. But this did not last long. Both my English and my American publishers offered to pay me to go to Capri, there to write a biography of Norman Douglas, whom I knew slightly and who agreed. So in November 1948 I sailed with my wife, third class, to Naples. We spent almost all our time in the first class bar, drinking with Sinclair Lewis, who was making his last transatlantic journey.

Norman Douglas was then eighty years old and had drunk heavily all his life. My drinking on Capri did not seem at all excessive. I have written elsewhere how we used to work on the biography, and I shall quote myself:

> The method of work we had devised, and which still seems to me in retrospect theoretically excellent, was as follows. In the mornings I would write. Apart from the sacred hour of the *siesta*, I would spend the afternoons with Norman. Our conversation would give me enough to work on next morning. When the first draft of each chapter was typed, I would show it to him and he would correct any errors of fact and suggest any misinterpretation of these that might have occurred to him. The evenings were left open. By this method, and at the rate I work, we estimated that the whole operation would take some six months.

> So we would set off, Norman and I, to a remote wine shop, quite unvisited by tourists, called the Arco Naturale. It was a long walk, the second half along an earthen track better adapted to the hooves of goats than to the feet of men. It was well worth the walk. As its name implies, it was a natural cave

and little more, with a couple of tables to one side. In front of us and across the water lay the mountains and tip of the Sorrentine Peninsula, upon which fell the rays of the afternoon and later of the setting sun. It was a place of extreme natural beauty, and we almost always had it to ourselves. The wine was cheap and rough but excellent, the real Capresi from grapes grown by the husband of the woman who served it, not the muck from the nearby island of Ischia which, in those days, was called Tiberio, labelled "made in Capri" and sold at exorbitant prices to foreigners. There were *bambini,* who deserved a sip of wine, maybe an orange, occasionally a very small banknote, for there were then no current coins of any value—even the small banknotes were still often grimy old pieces of paper issued for the armies of occupation.

There we sat for bottle after bottle. Occasionally a hunter, a *cacciatore* to be more exact, would pass on his homeward way from shooting birds, almost always sparrow-sized birds, finches and the like. Norman usually asked to see the day's bag. Usually sparrows. Once a hoopoe, once, I think to remember, a rock-creeper. "They will soon be extinct here," he remarked, with neither gloom nor amazement, for it was a sad statement of fact, and nothing more. So, too, was a remark he once made to me: "I wish you had known me when I was younger. I am only a husk, these days." There was no self-pity in it, nor did he expect or get a denial from me. He did not seem "a husk", but then I had never known him except in his old age. The man I knew was excellent company, witty and informative, if anything sometimes almost too strenuous for me, fifty years his junior. So there we sat, and there we talked until the shadows rose up the flanks of the mountains across the water. Or rather he talked while I listened and occasionally asked a question.

I am no Boswell. I made few notes (and those I no longer have) of our conversations. Furthermore, after several bottles of wine, when the sun was setting across the water and only the peaks were still lit, Norman would say:

"Ha! Time for a drink."

We would make our way, rather slowly, back to the village, to the Piazza at this hour, and Norman would order two large

dry martinis. These would be sent back, untasted, with in-
structions that they be made with English gin. After a few
minutes the drinks, the same drinks I have no doubt, would be
set before us. And so the evening began. Is it surprising that
the next morning my memory of what had been said was impaired, that I too tended to feel "skuimpy", and that the book
took much longer to write than I had anticipated? Perhaps he
really wished it to be that way.

This was the second book in a row that I had failed to finish,
the second millionaires' paradise on which I had gone broke. My
last few months on Capri were penniless and miserable. I arrived
in London, having left my wife in Rome, where she had a rather
vague job dubbing films, in December 1949, and with twopence
in my pocket. Old friends helped me over the worst. And rather
to my surprise, when my second novel was at last published, one
newspaper headlined its review with MEET THE POET OF
HANGOVER SQUARE. I suppose that there must be a lot
about drink in *The Iron Hoop*, written, it even then seemed,
years before, in Bermuda, but I had not noticed this, nor have I
reread it to find out.

Early in 1950 we rented a cottage in Hertfordshire, and I obtained work as a translator. We lived at Sacomb's Ash for over
nine years, during which time I translated some thirty books
from German, French, and Italian and wrote approximately one
book of my own each year.

Life there was very simple and regular. I would work all
morning. At about midday I would usually walk or cycle the half
mile to the village pub or walk a mile across the fields to the pub
in the next village, Green Tye, drink a couple of pints of bitter,
and walk home. We had no car, and on the rare occasions when
I had to go to London I would cycle to the nearest town,
Sawbridgeworth, and catch either the bus or the train. In the
evenings we would usually, but not invariably, go to the village
pub. We had a pin (a thirty-two-pint barrel) of bitter at home,
which lasted some two weeks. Very rarely—usually if we had
guests—we would buy a bottle of spirits, but these guests, know-
ing our poverty, generally brought one with them. Sometimes,
but certainly not invariably, we would get drunk on weekends.

Once I recall being sick at lunchtime: it was the occasion when I tasted the Chinese gin referred to earlier. I had no blackouts, never passed out as did one or two of our guests, and did not suffer from hangovers. I suppose I drank on the average about six pints of beer a day. Mowing the lawn, playing croquet, and the walks across the fields were my exercise. I recall mood swings, but no protracted depressions—though constantly short of money—and until very near the end only rare personality changes when in drink, though these had started, occasionally, much earlier, at least as early as Capri and usually took the form of jealous rows with my wife. People were somewhat taken aback by the amount of beer I drank on weekends, but nobody suggested I was an alcoholic. Most of my friends drank as much or more. On the other hand I certainly drank more than I could afford. We drank, in effect, all we could.

One protracted incident caused me periods of unhappiness and, eventually, of guilt. It should perhaps also have been a warning to me, but I did not take it as such.

My sister Mimi, of whom I was very fond, and her husband, of whom I was not, had always drunk far more heavily than I. For many years I had found their company and that of their friends tedious in the extreme, concerning as it did mostly their hangovers and their degree of drunkenness the night before. When I was on Capri she at last, and in my opinion belatedly, divorced him and came out to stay with me. She was an expensive guest, and I persuaded her to take a very small cottage on the beach at Positano, across the water. She was, I suppose, rather stupid, with really no interests, but very beautiful and gay. When I returned to England, she remained in Italy, living with a waiter who has since become a prosperous hotelier. She drifted and drank, to Austria among other places, but it was to Paris that I was summoned with the news that she was in severe trouble.

She was in a fifth-rate Latin Quarter hotel, incoherent with drink, cut and bruised. She said she had been beaten up by Arabs. I paid her hotel bill and took her to the American Hospital in Neuilly, where she was dried out. The young doctor said it was a straightforward case of alcoholism, and advised me to take her back to London, to Dr. Dent, whom I have already quoted and who believed solely in the aversion treatment. I took her, for

one night, to my Paris hotel and locked her in her room, while I
went out. She was very shaky, but managed to get out, borrow
money from the hotel management, and get drunk again. I only
just found her in time, next morning, and had difficulty in getting her on to the plane. But I did so, and delivered her to Dr.
Dent in the Cromwell Road.

He believed *solely* in the aversion cure, which used to be
called the Keeley Cure: this consists in giving the alcoholic his or
her favorite drink accompanied by an injection that will cause
fearful, painful vomiting. He gave his patients no follow-up
treatment, nor did he prescribe Antabuse (which I shall describe
later). She came to stay with me, shaky but determined not
to drink. She tried to get a job, selling apple juice, but without
much success. She was forever telephoning me, or turning up
with various men, which I did not care for. But she was not
drinking. Nor do I believe that she was doing so in secret, for
like me she had never been ashamed of her habits, as her pa-
thetic diary shows. She rented a cottage in Hampshire, much to
my relief. Early in the following year—it must have been about
1957—a hospital telephoned me that she was asking for me. It
was too far to go, and I was becoming tired of looking after her.
Next day the hospital telephoned me again. She had died of a
liver complaint. So I went to Hampshire, to identify her, collect
her few miserable possessions, and arrange her funeral. I told
myself that it would have made no difference if I had gone a day
earlier, but I could not help feeling that I had somehow betrayed
her, and I was very unhappy for a long time.

(It seems her ex-husband had visited her, and had persuaded
her to drink. After a protracted binge she was in hospital, and he
had disappeared. I have never heard of him since, and hope I
never do again.)

My ex-wife tells me that I had long suffered from occasional
personality changes when drunk, as long ago as Italy, becoming
suddenly nasty, particularly of course to her. I had become gay
and merely foolish in drink in the early years of our marriage.
Now, however, these personality changes became much more
frequent, almost regular, though of course I was not getting
drunk every night or even every weekend. I do not know

whether this acceleration of personality changes, which in my mind corresponds with my sister's death, was in fact in any way connected with it, or with the acute depression that followed. Probably not. But I do know that it then began to worry me, and I quite correctly associated it with drink, though I do not recall that I made any particular effort to cut down. I also became involved in a somewhat foolish love affair and once had just such a personality change with my mistress, treating her precisely as if she were my wife and accusing her of unfaithfulness to me with her husband. I must have become quite intolerable, for in 1959 my wife left me. We have since become good friends, and she has confirmed much of what I have here written. I did not wish her to leave me, and urged her to come back, but felt no real resentment. As I have said, according to my code of sexual morals, she was basically a free agent in my eyes once our marriage was over.

At no time did I suffer from the type of blackouts which some authorities see as a sure and indeed an inevitable symptom of alcoholism in the prodromal phase.

Indeed, I added a question mark to this chapter's title, for I do not seem to have gone through the symptoms of the prodromal phase, but to have landed, rather suddenly, in the middle of the crucial phase. But for the sake of others let me give what one authority lists as the four principal symptoms of the prodromal phase:

1. The company is drinking too slowly, the alcoholic sneaks extra drinks in other parts of the bar, or orders double measures. Inclined to gulp his drinks.
2. Preoccupation with alcohol, drinks before events at which alcohol will be available, and tries to ensure a supply following the event.
3. Develops guilt feelings about drinking, and avoids discussion on alcohol addiction. Makes promises (mainly to himself) about drinking, and minimizes the quantity taken.
4. Blackouts or alcoholic amnesia occur in the frequency of two out of ten drinking bouts.

Let me therefore go straight on to the crucial phase, though here again many of the symptoms do not seem, as will be shown, to correspond with my own story.

CHAPTER XVII

The "Crucial" Phase

Before going on to the symptoms associated with the next, or "crucial," phase, and also to the next phase of my alcoholic's autobiography with its first really severe crisis, there are three terms that require elucidation.

The first of these is the "blackout," which is supposed to be a sure sign of alcoholism in its early stages. This is a very clearly defined phenomenon. It involves temporary amnesia when drinking. Beyond a certain point in the evening, the man or woman will remember nothing. When in this state of amnesia he or she will usually behave quite normally, allowing for the amount of drink taken. But next day it will all be a blank and often the first question to pass the individual's lips will be: "Where is the car?" "But you drove it home." Since by definition one in five of those driving late at night, particularly on such occasions as New Year's Eve or over the Christmas holidays, will be in a state of temporary amnesia, and though in apparently full control of his faculties must have slow reactions and possibly faulty vision, it is hardly surprising that after the festivities many a road and particularly in the suburbs will be littered with smashed cars, and will sometimes resemble a battlefield.

I have never suffered from such blackouts in my life, though of course my memory is often faulty and at times positively misleading.

What is not listed, curiously, is passing out. This means falling into a coma, and is obvious to all. A man came down to Sacomb's Ash once to stay with me and passed out twice in the course of one evening. He had arrived with a bottle of whiskey at about six o'clock. He drank almost all of it himself, and fell off his chair, dead to the world. I lugged him upstairs and put him on his bed, removed his shoes and loosened his collar, and then my wife and I had dinner alone together. At about eleven Charles reappeared, and asked, somewhat shakily, for a drink. He refused any food, and drank nearly all of my bottle of whiskey. Toward midnight he passed out again, and once more I lugged this corpse-like figure up the stairs. We went to bed and at about 3 A.M. were awakened by his stumbling footsteps. I decided to take no further notice of him, and presumably he eventually found his own way back to bed, for there were no more spirits in the house. I may add that a couple of weeks later he committed suicide.

To the best of my knowledge I have never passed out, though I may have done so immediately after getting myself to bed. I believe that I was once or twice helped to undress but this can only have been very seldom.

What I have done is to faint, usually coming to before I hit the ground or else as soon as I did so. I am not sure, but suspect, that these fainting fits (which a doctor once described to me as epilepsy of the throat, and negligible) may be connected with alcohol, but more probably with smoking. Certainly the first time this happened I was entirely sober. I was indeed typing, and I can remember precisely what I was working at. It was the introductory passage to *The Shirt of Nessus*, which I wrote after finishing the body of the book. The date must therefore have been late 1955 or early 1956. It was in the morning, and I was horrified by what I had to type. I fainted. Some months later the telephone rang. It was a call with, for me, great emotional overtones, and quite unexpected, for my mistress and I had agreed never to telephone one another. When I heard her voice I again fainted. Later these fainting fits occurred more frequently, almost always after a bout of severe coughing and when I had been drinking, and smoking, heavily. So far as I remember they never happened when I was on the wagon, nor have I had one since I gave up drink altogether. They left me feeling, for a short time, rather shaky and, if in someone else's house or a public place, embarrassed. Apart from that I was able to con-

tinue as before. They occurred with increasing frequency. I
have never known anyone else to suffer from such fainting fits,
though perhaps that is why people fall off barstools. I have
fallen off two, and two only, in my life.

The next phase, which has not so far occurred in this list of
symptoms, is "personality change." This is very common, indeed
almost normal, among very heavy drinkers. I have already referred to it, and the reader will know it, or know *of* it. "He is a
regular Jekyll and Hyde character," a wife will remark. "When
he's sober he's so sweet, but when he drinks he becomes another
person, a real beast." Robert Louis Stevenson must either have
suffered from this or known intimately someone who did. With
me it has, I think invariably, been directed against the woman
I love, not against friends. It started, very occasionally, quite
early on in my drinking life, certainly no later than the Capri
period, and usually, though not invariably, when I was alone with
her, sometimes immediately after the departure of dinner guests
with whom I had appeared to be adequately sober. The change
is almost instantaneous and usually starts, as it were, in the middle
of a non-existent quarrel. (But this must be distinguished from
the ordinary quarrel that occurs in almost every marriage.) In
my case it almost always took the form of sexual jealousy, almost
invariably groundless, and in direct transference of my own personality defects to the woman I loved. It is explicable in the
framework of the three great modern psychologists. It is the
Freudian unconscious, liberated from its proper place by the
dulling of the superego and the ego; it is the Adlerian inferiority
feeling seeking compensation in stupid bullying; it is the Jungian
shadow persona emerging from the dark place that is its proper
home. With me it very seldom assumed the form of physical violence. On the other hand, it occurred with ever increasing repetition and what I said was highly repetitive. Since I did not suffer
from blackouts, I would remember and, next morning, apologize.
By the end I was apologizing almost every morning.

The third word that is much used in discussing drinking habits
is rationalization or its original verb, to rationalize. This verb
means "to render rational," a highly praiseworthy occupation,
since one of the principal functions of the brain is to see a pat-

tern, to connect cause with effect, to understand the meaning of
what at first glimpse may appear to be meaningless but is not.
To rationalize one's behavior is to make that behavior reasonable. However, in connection with drink, the word has come to be
used in precisely the opposite sense by people who should know
better. Its use—and this usage has become so common that I fear
I must use it here—has come to make it mean "finding a false excuse," the excuse being in its turn used to justify drinking. Thus:
"What a beastly cold day. It calls for a large whiskey." Or:
"What a lovely hot day. Let's have a drink." In this sense, or non-
sense, almost any event or emotion or incident can provide the
excuse, genuinely believed by the drinker, for one or many
drinks. Happiness or unhappiness, tiredness or a feeling of
abounding energy, boredom or excitement, a parting or a reun-
ion, travel or staying at home, a funeral or a christening, all call
for a drink. I myself have seldom bothered to rationalize. If I
want a drink, I will usually take one, or go to the pub. But I
have rationalized walks to the pub as exercise. And, to use the
unpleasant word the other way around, I have rationalized a day
in bed with a bottle of whiskey as a cure for a non-existent flu,
always of course believing what I say to myself or to others. And
the cleverer one is, the more convincing will such rationalizations be, at least to oneself but often to others. The only
thing they have in common is that they all end up with drink.

There are, however, exceptions. Perhaps the best known rationalization cliché is the drunk in the bar, justifying his prolonged presence there:

"My wife does not understand me."

This may well be quite true. A lot of women do not understand their husbands, even less so if he goes out Dr. Jekyll and
comes home Mr. Hyde. And possibly more men do not understand their wives.

Let me now return to my skeletal autobiography.

When Theodora left me, in the summer of 1959, I was upset
and urged her, in vain, to return. But she would not, so I in-
stigated divorce proceedings, for the simple reason that I did not
wish her to divorce me and obtain alimony, and I assumed, cor-

rectly, that she had found another man whom she preferred to myself.

I did not drink more, but rather less, when she had gone. I had found, or to be more exact Theodora had found, an old friend, not a mistress, to keep house for me, and I worked extremely hard at a novel, which I wrote in less than three months. I showed it to my publisher, Desmond Flower, who assured me that *When the Kissing Had to Stop* would sell very well. He was right, for it had and still does, a large new paperback edition having appeared very recently.

With that book completed, though it would not be published until the spring, I found the prospect of a whole winter alone in the country depressing. I did not, however, sell Sacomb's Ash (which I had recently bought on a mortgage) but rented a one-room flat, with bath and kitchen, in London, while Leona continued to keep house for me in the cottage so that I could go there whenever I chose.

In fact I spent very little time in London, partly because I drank—I almost wrote "inevitably" drank, a rationalization—more than pleased me. (Dylan Thomas used to call his boozy visits to London "the capital punishment.") It was in London that I met Marion.

A few days later I went to Wiltshire, to spend Christmas with my aunt. I came down with a very bad case of infectious hepatitis (jaundice) and after a time in the London Clinic went back to Sacomb's Ash to convalesce. Marion more or less nursed me, driving down from London every day, but dared not stay, as she was divorcing her husband. For six months I was on the wagon, by doctor's orders, and it was during this time that we fell in love. In fact she fell in love with a teetotaler, though this was certainly no pretense on my part, for I was merely obeying doctor's orders. Nor did I find it any hardship to abstain from all alcoholic drinks.

I remember that I took my first drink in June, the day she and I left for Berlin, where I had to attend an international conference of the Congress for Cultural Freedom.

Alcoholism is a progressive disease, whether the drinker drinks or not. If he stays on the dry for ten years, he will be no more "cured" than if he had been drinking all that time. Therefore, my disease was merely six months advanced when I began to drink again. And in Berlin, one night, I had precisely the same "personality change" that I had had before. I became extremely jealous because she had gone to see some old friend while I was busy with congressional matters. This should have been a warning both to her and, perhaps even more so, to myself. But we were very much in love, and we ignored it. Nor did it recur for some years.

Sacomb's Ash was too small for her and her two small daughters. I sold it at a considerable profit, bought and rapidly resold a large house in Dorset, again at a huge profit. My new novel was making quite a lot of money, and I did not hesitate to buy Waterston Manor, a large and very beautiful house near Dorchester. We were married that summer and a year later, in 1961, to my great joy she bore me a son. We were extravagant, or to be more exact I was. I still had my pin of beer, but I now also bought whiskey by the case. At one time we had a butler, who brought me each evening, at six sharp, a large whiskey and soda on a silver tray. I did not worry about money, largely because I assumed I had "arrived" and that my future books would sell as well as my last one. But it had been a fluke. My next novel was a flop. Money troubles were looming over the horizon and the upkeep of Waterston was clearly beyond my means. I drank too much, and the old symptoms reappeared in an aggravated form. We entertained a great deal, which in my case always meant heavy drinking.

If I have any reproach to make to Marion, it is that she did not understand the nature of my disease. Nobody else in the household—the Nanny, the other servants, her daughters—ever saw me the worse for drink.

Then, in 1962, I was asked to write the authorized life of Dylan Thomas, which I had earlier refused to do. I now agreed, for the sake of the money. This involved much travel and, as was perhaps really unavoidable with Dylan's friends, much drinking. The rows with Marion became worse and were almost invariably of my creation. I was now verging on the violent, though never beyond once or twice taking her by the shoulders and shaking her. Once she locked me out of our bedroom, and I broke down the door. Yet all this time I was working hard at an extremely difficult book.

The day after I had finished my *Life of Dylan Thomas,* on New Year's Eve, 1964/5, we went to London, a cocktail party and a dinner party. I got very drunk. Back at the hotel we had yet another row, and she walked out. I returned to Dorset the following day, assuming that she would follow. Instead, two days later, I received a solicitor's letter by which she informed me that she was taking out divorce papers.

I shall not go through the miseries of the divorce action, which I was prepared to defend, for I did not wish to lose my son. I was told that I would lose him in any case, whether I won or lost, and that I would also have to foot the bill or most of it. In some ways it was all really a gross misunderstanding, or so she told me a year later. The lawyers had stampeded her into it (at a cost of some five thousand pounds to myself), and she regretted it all. But I could not remarry her. I had passed through too much bitterness and had, indeed, developed cataracts in both eyes. I was selling Waterston, which I had loved so much, and had almost resolved to leave England. The basis of Marion's divorce action had been my drunkenness. This then seemed to me silly. Now I realize it was correct. I was becoming impossible to live with, or at least for her to live with. The rows would have begun again. I appreciated, and still appreciate, her attitude. And I see now that it was not me she had divorced, but my shadow persona. Mrs. Jekyll had divorced Mr. Hyde. If I failed to understand this at the time, it is hardly surprising that she should have believed, quite correctly, that Dr. Jekyll was the real me. Unfortunately, though, Mr. Hyde had been making considerable progress. I gave myself all sorts of good reasons for leaving England, but perhaps behind them all, and certainly unknown to me, was the unexpressed longing that I might leave Mr. Hyde behind. I spent a winter in Ireland, alone save for a secretary-housekeeper, tucked away in a cottage in West Cork, where I drank very little and worked very hard. The sales of my *Dylan Thomas* were excellent and I got a high price for Waterston. The alimony I had to pay was minimal, though I increased this greatly, for the sake of my son. I made quite frequent visits to Dublin, where I had many friends. These, though, verged on "the capital punishment," but Dublin is a much smaller capital city than London. My eyes were getting worse, operations inevitable. Nevertheless I returned to England, in the spring of 1966, a healthier man. But I had decided that I would make my new home in Ireland. I had no intention of establishing any permanent relationship with any woman ever again. I said as much to my mother.

Let us now examine the far more numerous symptoms of The Crucial Phase. Many of these, as will be seen, do not apply to me, but may to you, the reader, or to someone with whom you are deeply concerned. They are numbered. I shall give the symptom in italics, my comments in normal print.

1. *Loss of control.* I take it that this refers to control over alcoholic intake. In which case I would say that by the middle of the Waterston period I was pouring myself drinks without noticing it. If it means loss of control generally, I do not feel that I ever did lose control, save during periods of "personality change."

2. *Rationalization of drinking behavior.* A certain amount of this, as already stated. The most important rationalization, however, comes later in this book, a rooted conviction that I needed "a certain amount" to drink in order to write easily and well.

3. *Social pressures, reproved by family, friends, employer.* My way of life did not make me subject to social pressures, for I had no wish to mix in "society." Nor had I an employer. Some publishers try to treat their authors as employees: such publishers do not last long, because they very rapidly have no authors of any value. My friends usually drank about as much as myself, but I do recall Basil Liddell Hart, who was a generation older than me, once warning me that I should watch out with the drink. This must have been about 1963, on one of the many occasions when I was staying with him. And at a slightly later date my mother told me once that I stank like a distillery. She never said anything like this to me before or since, which is why it has stuck in my memory.

4. *Grandiose behavior.* When I bought Waterston Manor an

aged uncle warned me of the danger of being "overhoused," a word that was new to me. I have always tended to live beyond my means. I have never, I trust, strutted about and shown off peacock-fashion, which is how I should describe grandiose behavior.

5. *Occasional morning drinking.* Not occasional but perpetual, virtually from the time I started to drink, save when on the wagon.

6. *Marked aggressive behavior.* I do not believe so, though perhaps I have always expressed myself more forcefully than most people. On very rare occasions I have been, deliberately, extremely rude, but this has not been in any way progressive or indeed really connected with drink at all.

7. *Persistent remorse.* No.

8. *Periods of total abstinence.* Save for the post-hepatitis period described in this chapter, and periods in my army career—that is to say enforced abstinence—none until a later stage, described in the next chapter.

9. *Attempts to ration intake.* Very feeble and occasional up to this point, being usually little more than the temporary substitution of beer for spirits.

10. *Drops friends.* No. My friends and I have sometimes drifted apart, but that is quite another matter.

11. *Quits job.* This would mean, in my case, "stops writing." I have never stopped writing.

12. *Behavior becomes alcohol centered, avoids activities which interfere with drinking.* The only such activity which occurs to me is that I more or less gave up going to the theater and the cinema, unless there was something I particularly wanted to see. The protracted waste of drinking time in order to watch a dull play or film certainly contributed to this. It may even have been the main cause. On the other hand, this can hardly apply to TV in my own home, which I have usually felt a marked reluctance to watch, drunk or sober, because it is usually, to me, so boring.

13. *Loss of outside interests.* No. Rather the contrary. My interests, outside literature and the arts, were always very small. In the late 1950s I became increasingly interested in world politics and also in history and metaphysics.

14. *Reinterpretation of interpersonal relationships.* I do not know what this gobbledegook means. Perhaps it refers to the breakup of my marriages.

15. *Marked self-pity—suicide attempts significant.* I have always and quite consciously avoided any form of self-pity. Not only were there no suicide attempts, but suicide was never even contemplated. Only if my entire drinking career is regarded as one long, masked attempt at self-destruction (which I do not believe is the case) has this item any relevance.

16. *Geographic escape.* My departures from Bermuda and from Italy were in a way an escape, but not from drink. My departure from England to Ireland was certainly connected with a desire to change my way of life. However, Ireland was, and has remained, a far pleasanter country for me to live in. I have roots here, as I have in America. In England I have friends, which is not at all the same thing. But on the whole I think that my deliberate and long-considered move to Ireland could be considered as an escape in this context.

17. *Change in family habits.* My divorces, that is all.

18. *Resentments.* None, save quite briefly toward Marion during the divorce period.

19. *Protects supply.* Most certainly so. Whenever I could afford it, and sometimes when I could not, I kept an ample supply of various drinks in the house. And I would have hated to live beyond walking distance from a pub, bar, or café.

20. *Neglects proper nutrition.* Again the answer is positive. I became, probably on Capri if not before, a finicky and difficult man to feed, known for my sparrow-like appetite. As early as 1938 I remember discussing with a friend how pleasant it would be if one could only take a pill instead of having to sit through a whole meal. Theodora, who is the author of numerous cookbooks, found me extremely difficult to feed at the end. When drinking I would often prefer a sandwich to a meal, or even on occasion nothing at all.

21. *First admission to hospital.* This occurred later, and will be discussed in the next chapter.

22. *Decrease in sexual drive.* Not, I think, what was beyond the normal aging process, particularly remembering that as a young man my sexual drive had been markedly pronounced.

This was not a symptom in the period of which I have been writing.

23. *Alcoholic jealousy*. Extremely pronounced, and from a very early stage, as this book has shown.

24. *Regular morning drinking*. Always, when available.

This schema, by the way, comes from *Medical Effects of Alcoholism*, compiled by the Irish National Council on Alcoholism, Dublin, a booklet undated but by the evidence of the bibliography presumably put together in 1974.

So this takes us to the spring of 1966, when I was forty-six years old, and had returned to London after spending a winter alone in Ireland. I had there nearly completed a volume of autobiography in which there is little reference to drink. I had a flat in London, which was temporarily let, and which I had furnished with such pieces from Waterston as I wished to keep. It had been redecorated for me, and bookcases built. Nanny had stayed on as my housekeeper and to look after Francis, my son, who spent his holidays with me. I had no other emotional entanglements, though in London quite a number of unemotional ones. My *Life of Dylan Thomas* was bringing in good money, and I had just been awarded a Guggenheim Fellowship, worth nine thousand dollars, to write a book about denazification, the material for which was almost entirely available in London's Wiener Library. I thought that I could live a carefree bachelor's life in London and also work, both at my books and at the documentary scripts which I was then writing quite regularly for the BBC. It was all quite possible, in theory.

In practice it was far more difficult. I drank heavily but discreetly, in part for Nanny's sake and also for that of my son, who told me, the other day, that he had never seen me the worse for drink in his life. (But he is now a tactful and well-mannered young man. He may have wished not to hurt me.) But I was getting fat, despite eating so little, and my weight had gone up to some two hundred pounds, which was a good thirty pounds overweight. My eyes were getting worse. I saw the best specialist, who said I must have cataract operations soon. I asked Mr. Duke Elder if there were a good eye surgeon in Dublin, and he assured me that Mr. Louis Werner was second to none in the world. (I was not on British National Health, being an American, and the whole British medical service was out of joint even then, with long delays and huge bills.)

Mr. Duke Elder was puzzled by my developing cataracts at so early an age. (They are hereditary. My mother had them, but in her seventies.) He said that they might well have been brought about prematurely by the nervous strain of my divorce. However, he also wanted me to see a diabetes expert.

I saw the diabetes man, who gave me a very thorough examination after the requisite hours of fasting. He told me that I had a mild diabetic condition and must take some pills called Rastinon. This I did for several years. He also told me that I drank too much. I was tempted to say that I did not need to come all the way to Harley Street in order to learn this. He gave me a regimen: two lagers or two glasses of light wine a day. I did not take this very seriously, indeed I rapidly paid no attention to it at all.

But I did go to see a drink expert, whose name I will omit. He was said to be the best in London, since Dr. Dent was dead. I had a long conversation with him and discovered that several of my friends had been his patients. He said, at last, that in his opinion I was not then an alcoholic, but could become one, and he advised me to watch my drinking carefully. When I asked that he get his secretary to prepare a bill he said:

"No. I have done nothing for you."

Surely an unheard of remark by a most distinguished doctor who had given me at least two hours of his time!

I was still worried about my health, particularly my diabetes and my weight. An acquaintance advised me to go to a health farm, a place called Enton Hall, from which she had just returned, having lost a lot of weight. I arranged to go there for three weeks, in April. And with that a new chapter of my life opened, as will a new chapter of this book.

CHAPTER XVIII

The Lengthy Crisis

The English health farm differed, and I believe still does, from the American variety, which is more a health-and-beauty farm usually organized by such firms as Elizabeth Arden. Champneys at Tring had been the first English one, created before the war and copied quite extensively—there must have been half a dozen of them in the 1950s. They were usually run by osteopaths, who were in general no longer distrusted as they had once been by the medical profession, and their purpose was not cosmetic but essentially to improve the patient's health, in particular by loss of weight. I have been to most of them and can confirm that in the 1960s and early 1970s Enton Hall lived up to its reputation of being the strictest of them all.

There were three main types of clients. The first comprised people in perfectly good health, such as jockeys, actors, and dancers who needed to lose weight for professional reasons. The second consisted of those, like myself, who were grossly over-weight through excessive eating and drinking, or who were sim-ply unwell, usually because of drink. The third comprised those, often businessmen or women, who needed a complete break with their normal life in order to rest.

The treatment consisted, basically, of a starvation diet, no drink, massage and sauna baths, infrared treatment, which was optional, occasional osteopathy, as much rest as possible and as much walking, too. Telephones were cut off at 10 P.M. Outings were permitted in the afternoon, to visit whatever the local sites of interest might be, or even to go into the neighboring country town for a cup of tea. The starvation diet was gradually relaxed, and the client given delicious mixed nut and vegetable salads, a sort of vegetarian smorgasbord.

Some people cheated, and went out to eat or even drink. This seemed to me extraordinarily stupid, since these places were far from cheap, and I always stuck entirely to the prescribed regimen. The conversation among the majority of the inmates, who were of both sexes, was unusually dull, being mostly about food. I walked and read a great deal, though the starvation produced not merely relaxation but also a sort of lethargy amounting to stupidity. I recall, for instance, that it took me most of one afternoon to write a perfectly simple short letter to a close friend. After the first twenty-four to forty-eight hours (during which I suffered none of the withdrawal symptoms that are supposed to accompany a sudden abandonment of alcohol) I had no desire whatsoever for a drink. After a week, during which I lost some fifteen pounds, I began to feel healthy and more interested in my fellow patients. In three weeks I lost close on thirty pounds, and emerged feeling very well indeed, better than I had in years. I resolved to take these cures—which must correspond in some ways to the old-fashioned cures at Baden-Baden, Vichy, or Saratoga Springs—regularly, and indeed did so for several years. They did not solve my alcoholic problem, nor presumably that of anyone else, but they certainly had a physiological effect in that they gave the abused body (and particularly the liver) a break and the mind a rest. (It was quite impossible to work at a health farm. I once tried to correct the proofs of a book in one: it was extraordinarily difficult, nor was this rather simple task well done.) Furthermore, since my diabetic condition was directly connected with my being overweight (though the experts had not then told me this), the loss of some thirty pounds in three weeks must have been good for me.

It was at Enton Hall that I met Marjorie, and once the first week was over I spent a great deal of time with her. Our walks through the woods were long and lovely. She was very beautiful, an American some ten years younger than myself, and was there for a rest from drinking. She had been married twice, once to a multimillionaire and then, giving up an alimony of about a quarter million pounds a year, to an actor whom she was divorcing.

We discussed our private affairs, our marriages, and our drink problems, but not all the time. She had been a star in the American and British theater, but really regarded herself as a painter, and had had exhibitions in London, New York, and elsewhere. Like me, she was then at a completely loose end, without a home and indeed without any real desire as to where she wished to live. She had two children in their teens by her first marriage, and one boy of three by her second. She also had a certain amount of capital, but was not quite sure how much. Her affairs were handled by a multitude of lawyers and accountants, from London to Los Angeles, of varying efficiency. She also had a secretary/companion, who was not with her at Enton Hall. Marjorie was clearly in a complete mess, both emotionally and financially.

It must not be imagined that we discussed our private affairs in any depth. On the contrary, we laughed a great deal together, at the Enton Hall system and the other inmates, at the Watts collection, which we had visited, at my reminiscences of Dylan Thomas (she had read my life of the poet), at much else. Our relationship developed fast, in complete sobriety, nor did I try to make love to her, though tempted so to do and well aware that I should not be rebuffed. For us both this was a period of disinvolvement rather than involvement, and for me this was emphasized when Marion visited me, with Francis, for a day's picnic in the woods. The nearest Marjorie and I came to any commitment, and this was only a vague one, was that she decided tentatively that she too would buy a house in Ireland, near mine, when I should have bought my own.

She had arrived at Enton Hall a few days earlier than I had, and therefore left for a London hotel while I still had to complete my "cure." The next day she telephoned me from London some twenty-five times, in a condition of steadily increasing intoxication, until finally I rang off in mid-conversation, if such it could by then be called, and told the telephone operator to accept no further calls for me.

I then made certain calculations. She had admitted she was an alcoholic, and therefore would hardly reproach me if I drank too much. She was desperately lonely and some of her advisers were, I had realized, very unreliable. For two weeks at Enton Hall she had never cheated: that she should get drunk on her return to London, alone in a strange hotel, did not shock or even particularly surprise me. I was apparently her only friend, and it was possible that in drink she imagined herself in love with me. It would be priggish in the extreme for me to reproach her.

And the ghost of Mimi rose to haunt me. I was only too well aware, and recently, of the miseries of a British divorce action. Also, she was extremely attractive, not merely physically but because of an innate modesty. Few women, in my opinion, could have been a star of the stage, a moderately successful painter, and a millionairess without becoming in some way spoiled. Yet she was not spoiled at all. When sober she was extremely good company, entertaining, open-minded, not self-centered. But beneath all that I sensed, particularly in her drunkenness on the telephone, a profound despair. (I did not then know that her father had been a drunkard who had killed himself.) On the one hand I felt strongly attracted to her; on the other I felt that I might help her over this crisis in her life. In order to do this, I knew that I must become her lover, but the prospect certainly did not displease me. I would, on the other hand, never have believed that a year later we would be married, a year after that the parents of a daughter, and that twelve years later I should be writing this book with Marjorie in the next room, for at that time I had no wish to marry, or to live with, her or any other woman.

When I returned to London we immediately became lovers and I discovered that her affairs were in even worse shape than I had suspected. I arranged that she rent a house in the country (at a vastly inflated rent), and that she be reunited there with her little son, Peter, just a year younger than my own. (He had been boarded out with a nice but useless and pregnant Irish girl.) There she had another drinking bout, and I nearly walked out. Indeed I did walk out, in a way, but now I also had the responsibility of little Peter. Since it was term time and Francis was with his mother, I left Nanny with Marjorie to look after Peter. I began to sort out her divorce.

When she was better I took her to Ireland with me, having arranged to sell the lease of my London flat. We spent a very happy ten days there, drinking as I thought normally (which

meant quite heavily), seeing my friends in Dublin, and traveling
down to West Cork, to look at a house on Bantry Bay which I
thought of renting. There was still no question of our living together. The plan now was that she would rent a Dublin house, so
that between us we would have a town and a country residence.
We found her one, and I liked the West Cork one, Tregariff. I
took it, as of September 1, and she signed a lease for the Dublin
house from the same date, each for one year.

She did not have a drunken bout, ending in a personality
change and unconsciousness such as I had seen in England. It
was, in fact, the last time that she was able to drink normally,
though I had assumed that she was on the road to recovery. We
were very happy together, and I was falling in love with her. I
saw my Irish eye surgeon, Louis Werner, and it was agreed that
I have my first cataract operation in November, my second some
months later. I would use her Dublin house as my base for these.

Back in England, it was time for Francis's holidays. I had
rented a house in Dorset for these, and was able to employ our
old cook, thus, I hoped, giving him the maximum of continuity.
Marjorie had been joined by her teen-age daughter, on holiday
from a finishing school in Switzerland. She was a beautiful,
charming, and, it seemed, responsible girl. With her son, whom I
did not then meet, her daughter, and, I think, little Peter, but
without me, Marjorie revisited Ireland and decided she was
doing the right thing in taking the Dublin house. Once she came
down to see me in Dorset, and all went well. While in England
she telephoned me, or I her, almost every day. Only once, I
think, was she drunk. The presence of her elder son was always a
sobering influence, as was Francis with me.

When her two elder children had gone back to their schools,
she moved over to Ireland with her secretary and Peter. I followed a few days later, but spent only a couple of nights in
Dublin, partly because I had taken a strong dislike to the secretary, partly because I wished to get down to West Cork and
write as much as I could of my denazification book before I had
my operations, for I knew I would be more or less blind for several months.

I had been there, with Nanny once again my housekeeper, for

only a week or so when Marjorie telephoned me, very drunk, and told me incoherently how unhappy she was. I therefore rang friends who lived nearby and whom I had asked to keep an eye on Marjorie. They reported almost immediately that she was in a more or less perpetual coma, that Peter was being neglected, and that the legal executive who was dealing with her affairs had arrived and wanted her to sign various papers. I arranged with my friends that they send Peter, by car, to Nanny's sister in Athlone (where Francis had lived during part of my own divorce action), and I told Marjorie to get a car at once and come to West Cork. I felt this was preferable to myself going to Dublin and meeting the legal executive and the secretary.

The legal executive appeared to object to my intervention. I only learned she was en route to West Cork when the secretary telephoned me and told me more. "What," she asked, "would I be wanting with a stupid drunken woman?" I took it upon myself to tell her there and then that she was fired and so was the legal executive. A few hours later Marjorie arrived, shaken and exhausted but sober and, I think, happy to be freed of all responsibilities, which I willingly accepted. I arranged that a lawyer known to me obtain her divorce, and began to clean up her affairs. This seemed so nearly impossible that at one point I suggested it would be simpler if she simply gave her California property to her mother, who was in any event already living there, and everything else to charity. However, by engaging lawyers known to me in Dublin and New York, I was at last able to make some sense of her affairs. And she wasn't drinking.

It was a grim winter for her and for me, but worse I think for her. She told me that she knew she must give up drinking, but she asked me not to do so on her account. She had no desire to make me miserable too. Nor had I, and I was touched by her attitude. Meanwhile it was agreed that it would be best if, for some months, Peter remained in Athlone, where she visited him from time to time.

She then told me about her drinking career, though what follows is obviously both simplified and amplified by what she has told me at later dates.

She was one of four sisters, born in Reno, Nevada, and

brought up in hillbilly country and in San Francisco. Her father was half Red Indian, and it is to this heritage that she ascribes, in large measure, both her own and his alcoholism. For he had gotten drunk, regularly, on weekends, which he usually ended in a police cell. However, he was a good worker and never lost a job, though frequently changing his employment and even his type of work. Her mother was of predominantly Scandinavian origin, very pretty and very respectable. Marjorie's parents— their name was Steele, which she used during her theatrical career—quarreled frequently and bitterly in front of the children. Marjorie began working at an early age, menial jobs in shops and so on, but managed to win a scholarship to a drama school. She was taken up by Constance Collier, who believed in her talents and really gave her what education both as a person and as an actress she acquired in her youth. She learned to paint by working with an art restorer. She married an extremely rich man at a very early age, and soon had two children. Her first husband hardly drank, and until about the age of twenty-five, that is to say some ten years before I met her, she too drank lightly and normally, for she knew by experience that after four or five drinks she would black out.

She can give no explicit reason for what was almost an overnight change, save perhaps her way of life. She was then playing the lead, in New York and on the road, in *Cat on a Hot Tin Roof,* traveling coast to coast for about a year, usually flying home on weekends to see her husband and children in one of his many houses. In California during this tour she took to drinking heavily, alone in her hotel room, after the show. On one occasion at least she smashed up the hotel. This was the beginning of her secret drinking. Not that secrecy was in any way necessary, but like many woman alcoholics she preferred it that way. Nor was the secrecy successful, for she soon became an epsilon alcoholic: that is to say, one drink meant a bottle in an hour, personality change and violence in varying forms. Her marital relations with her husband, a notorious womanizer, had ceased. Her theatrical career became more difficult, though she never missed a performance and never turned up drunk. She learned to fly and took up skin diving in a big way, in part at least in a not altogether unsuccessful attempt to change her way of life. But the drinking bouts recurred. No cost was spared to cure her, the money being principally spent on psychoanalysts, who did her no good whatsoever, nor would she take the Antabuse that one doctor prescribed. She more or less gave up the theater and went back to painting, which was really her first love. The drinking bouts grew more frequent.

For some reason which I have never really understood—and have not asked, for it is basically no concern of mine, or of the reader—she decided to divorce her husband. He did not wish this, and the divorce was both protracted and painful. This, following on the suicide of her father, whom she had deeply loved, drove her more and more to the bottle. She was allotted by the judge the largest alimony ever then given in any American court, but much seems to have gone to the lawyers of both sides.

She had never been at all mercenary, and this she now proved by marrying a second time, thereby giving up her huge income, though she was not by any standards a poor woman, and her first husband continued to buy her paintings at good prices and from a quite genuine admiration for her work.

Marjorie rapidly realized that she had made a mistaken second marriage, but by then a child had been born. For a couple of years she tried, with the help of the bottle, to keep the marriage going. She was living in London now, painting a little, and was at about her lowest ebb when first I met her at Enton Hall. She fell very much in love with me, almost immediately.

Such was the background to her painful winter at Tregariff, when she tried—with no assistance either from me or from any medical source—to give up drinking, which is something I should advise no man or woman who has reached such a state ever to attempt.

She went through a period of anxiety (which is the clumsy medical translation of *Angst*) and this took with her a form of extreme fear, so that she scarcely dared speak to strangers. She has always cut her cables, and she seemed to have no friends: the people we saw were my friends or the one or two acquaintances we made in West Cork. This "cutting of cables" may be an exaggerated form of that geographical escape referred to in the previous chapter. Being a secret, or would-be secret, drinker, she did not wish to return to places such as hotels where she had been drunk or to see people who had, or even who might have, seen her drunk. I did not appreciate this silent fear, for after all I did not know her very well and falsely ascribed it to a becoming, indeed a pleasing, modesty. Besides, I was not seeing very much that winter, and she is a very good actress. She never let me even guess how much all the drink that was about distressed her.

For some three months I worked at my book on denazification, a dull subject I could hardly share with her, and at sorting out her affairs. She did not drink at all; I did at my normal rate but without any personality changes. Our sexual relations were very happy. She appreciated the regularity of our lives, perhaps above all else, for she had never before known it in her life, save for the technical regularity of hours provided by the theater. I think that this began to give her the feeling of security which almost all women need and want, but it did not outweigh the awful, illogical miseries of *Angst*.

In November I had my first eye operation, in a Dublin nursing home. Marjorie had come up with me, and bought a new car. In this she set off for Athlone, to see her son, Peter, but got drunk on the way. She had the sense to stop off at the house of friends, where she sobered up. We did not use the house she had rented, but stayed at a hotel, and soon drove back to Bantry Bay. My next operation was due in February and until then I was almost, but not quite, blind. I managed to do an hour's or so work a day, but for the rest listened mostly to my new record player and drank heavily, for there is a limit to the number of symphonies one can enjoy in a day. I recall an exceptionally miserable Christmas. My son, Francis, had come over for his holidays and Peter was back from Athlone. Francis went down with acute tonsilitis and the doctor said he must be operated on immediately, in Cork. His mother wished me to send him back to London, but the doctor said this would be unsafe. Then Marjorie had another drinking bout and had to be taken to hospital in Cork. Nanny and I managed to keep this from the boys. Francis returned to London, Peter to Athlone, and in February I had my second eye operation. This too was successful, and I quite rapidly regained the use of my eyes, behind thick and permanent spectacles.

In March, Marjorie went to New York. I resented this, because I was now beginning to feel proprietorial about her, in my case a sure if unattractive sign of love. It angered me when I telephoned her at her hotel and the secretary I had fired answered, to inform me that I could not speak to Marjorie, as she was in the bedroom with her first husband. Marjorie later told me that this was quite untrue. She had in fact gone to New York to see her two elder children, who were now both living there, and for the last time, since she intended to commit suicide by jumping from a high window. But the windows were hermetically sealed. Instead she arrived back, very drunk, sometime in April. I did not reproach her, or feel any anger, so great was my relief that she was safely home. Instead I took her to a health farm in England, which did us both temporary good, and then to Paris, which we both enjoyed. Long visits to the Louvre and other museums awakened in her a real desire to start painting seriously again. We also decided that we should get married and buy a house near Dublin, for we neither of us wished to spend another winter in West Cork.

Back in Ireland, we quite rapidly found the house in Killiney where I am writing this book, and bought it immediately. We would move in September, when my lease on the West Cork house ran out. That was in 1967. All four of the children spent a lovely summer holiday with us, on the shore of Bantry Bay, not yet polluted by the oil companies. We got married, and our daughter was born in 1968.

I shall say little more about Marjorie's drinking, for this really comes later. With numerous relapses at varying intervals and of varying intensities, she was at last helped to master her *Angst*, helped by Antabuse and by the careful attention of Dr. John Cooney, of St. Patrick's Hospital, Dublin. Antabuse also comes later. I myself took far longer to realize that my own condition, though utterly different from hers, was to become at least as serious.

CHAPTER XIX

To the Very Gates of Hell

By the nature of this book, it must seem that the past ten years of my life have been preoccupied with my own and Marjorie's alcoholism. This is quite misleading. We were both working hard, and usually well; we traveled quite a bit, usually together, sometimes alone, to Italy, to Paris, to Austria, three times to Greece, three times to the United States. I made frequent visits to London, and she to California and to the Virgin Islands, where her elder daughter was living. After our first visit to Greece, she took up sculpture, with which she has had a considerable success. I wrote half a dozen or more books, including a study in depth of the situation in Northern Ireland when the civil rights movement began there and I foresaw grave trouble. This involved considerable research into all aspects of Irish history. I also wrote a concise history of Germany, a short history of Ireland, and an even shorter life of Eamon de Valera, as well as at least three novels and much journalism. We entertained, and were entertained, as much as we wished. For my fiftieth birthday, in 1969, we gave a house party that lasted for the better part of a week. The details of our real life I omit, for this book is essentially a study of my alcoholic career. I do not keep a diary and so the dates that I shall give must be qualified and may well be wrong.

Marjorie was now being looked after by Dr. Cooney, who by what might be called, rather rudely, a system of trial and error had tracked down her alcoholism to acute depression and was giving her the appropriate medication, while she also derived much help from his "Thursday meetings," a sort of group therapy for alcoholics on the dry. She was worried by my own drinking, as was I, though I scornfully refused to admit that I could possibly be an alcoholic: I just drank heavily, as I had always done. But my tolerance for alcohol was decreasing. I was beginning to worry about going out to dinner, since on several occasions I had become very drunk, quite quickly, and had had to go home. Also I was increasingly suffering from "personality change" and turning foul-tempered (with Marjorie) at night. And I had, but only rarely, brief, partial blackouts.

I had long before developed two physical symptoms, neither of which I understood nor had had explained to me by the doctors. The first was a numbness in my middle toes. When having my first eye operation I asked that a GP come to see me about this. He said it was quite normal in a heavily built man of my age with a habit of pacing the room while at work. The other was an itchy rash on my back. A London doctor, in 1965, had prescribed something to put in my bath. I did so, when living a life of sobriety alone in West Cork. The rash vanished. Now it came back, and no dermatologist could explain or cure it. At last it was diagnosed as peripheral neuritis, a malady closely connected with alcoholism, as indeed were the numb toes. Both have vanished since I stopped drinking.

My diabetes, I was told, was connected with my being overweight. Frequent visits to health farms helped control my weight, and at one I had myself examined by a GP for diabetes. He found no trace of it—I had been on the wagon for two weeks —and told me that if I were diabetic and drank as much as I normally did I should probably be dead by now or at least would have had frequent and serious collapses, far beyond my fainting fits. He advised me to throw the Rastinon pills away, even though the Harley Street diagnosis had been confirmed by a Dublin specialist. I did so, about 1971, and there was no change in my general health. Nevertheless, when last I was in hospital, severe diabetes was diagnosed, but disappeared a few days later. I have been on a diabetic diet since, though I am more or less convinced that the appearance of the symptoms was connected with alcoholism. On the other hand, I have a sister who is a confirmed and severe diabetic, and diabetes does run in families. Besides, if one has given up drink, the rest of a diabetic's diet is no hardship whatsoever.

About a year later, Marjorie persuaded me to see Dr. Cooney. I did so, to please her, and told him my story as honestly as I could. I also told him that if I needed psychiatric treatment, which I imagined resembled psychoanalysis, I should rather not be treated by the same doctor as my wife. He understood, and asked me only one question: was I jealous? I replied very much so. It seemed to me then an odd and irrelevant question, though now I think I understand it. I asked him if he thought I was an alcoholic, and he replied that he did not know. I construed this —rationalization again—as meaning I was not. Therefore, when I went to see Professor Moore, who apparently took it for granted that I was, I dismissed the professor from my mind, and did not visit him again at that time. My condition continued to deteriorate and my depression to increase. I told myself that it was in order to please Marjorie, in her efforts to conquer her sickness, that I agreed on medical treatment. But I would on no account go to St. Patrick's, where I had visited her and perhaps been unfortunate in my reactions to the hospital. I therefore went, voluntarily but rather cynically, to their country branch, St. Edmondsbury. There I was given an injection, and immediately had a most violent attack of delirium tremens. I had never had the DTs before, or any marked withdrawal symptoms of any kind when making my numerous trips to health farms. I loathed this country hospital, where I had to walk down what seemed a very long corridor to the toilet. Once I did not make it, and fouled my pajamas, for me an almost unbearably humiliating experience. I left the place as soon as I could, after being given an intelligence test which I regarded as nonsensical. I agreed with Marjorie to cut out all drink for three months, a promise I kept though I wanted a drink all the time.

While on the dry I wrote a novel called *In the Bunker*. I have been told it is among my best, but I always denied this. I believe that this is a queer form of rationalization, for I had convinced myself that I could not write properly without at least a moderate intake of alcohol. Who had ever heard of a teetotal writer? Therefore my novel must be poor. Without rereading it, I think that my friendly critics were right and that I was wrong. But I place little trust in my literary judgment of my own books.

Because of the progressive nature of the disease, when I returned to drinking I was immediately much worse. I was now getting into a truly depressed state, which I euphemized as "cumulative exhaustion" and persuaded my GP to put me to sleep for three or four days. He did this, and for a while I felt better. This was about 1975, and I paid my last visit to a health farm. My stay was ruined, in part because when I telephoned home on my arrival Marjorie was drunk. Fortunately her elder son arrived in Ireland on the following day, so she did not have a bout. But I think I had progressed beyond the point at which a health farm routine could help me. I had no withdrawal symptoms, but one of the nurses found me in my room looking so ill and miserable that she insisted on bringing me tea and toast. The bill was outrageous, the osteopath (a new one) unsympathetic and I suspected inefficient.

Back home, I finished an extremely difficult book, *Secret Intelligence in the Twentieth Century*. I was aware, for the first time, that I was writing without my usual concentration of effort. The enormous research was superficial, not because I had not read the books but because my memory was becoming defective.

With the book finished, edited and ready for publication—which takes up to a year these days—I began a novel, but my heart was not in it, my depression increasing. In the spring of 1976 I had an alcoholic collapse at home and was taken by ambulance to St. Patrick's Hospital. There I was once again given an injection, and once again developed the DTs, though I think in retrospect that these must have begun in my workroom, at home. In any event, this was only the second time in my life that I had had them, both times following on or connected with a St. Patrick's injection. My rationalization now took the form that it was the injection, not the drink, that had given me the DTs. With ill grace I attended the compulsory lectures and had myself discharged as soon as possible. I did not go on the wagon, but I did cut down considerably on my drink intake. However, I also, and for the first time, began to cheat, though not much. I would sneak a double whiskey or a large vodka in the pub when my wife was not present. My legs were beginning to weaken, which worried me, and I attached more and more importance to my daily walk to the pub. However, my wife saw a certain improvement in my condition. I tried to continue my novel, but usually felt too tired to work. I was sleeping about twelve hours a day now, and anxious to get to the pub immediately after breakfast. Yet in November I was quite capable of going to London and making numerous recordings for radio concerning my forthcoming book.

I had expected great things of this book, and was bitterly disappointed that it was not better received. However, I was able, in January 1977, to make a most exhausting tour of the United States, promoting the book on TV and in press interviews. I was working or flying all day and every day for some three weeks, and was always entirely sober. Yet my publisher told me I had spent five hundred dollars on drinks in the various hotel bars. I did not believe him, and assumed the hotels had cheated him. Now I am not so sure. My friends assured me I had always appeared entirely sober on TV and, with one exception, in their company.

I arrived back in Ireland in late January, and the nightly rows began again. What has now become a very hazy year ensued. I tried, with no success, to work, to drink less, to improve my physical condition, which continued to deteriorate. In February of 1978, in order—Marjorie has told me—to frighten me, she deliberately got drunk and had to be taken off in her turn to St. Patrick's. This, however, did not stop me drinking, indeed quite the contrary, but it made me extremely unhappy. I drank now out of despair, about two or three bottles of whiskey a day, telling myself that I would go back to my limited intake when she returned from hospital. I could not. My legs had become so weak that I could hardly walk, and she had to drive me to the pubs, and even help me up the stairs. My doctor told me that I would soon be in a wheelchair if I went on this way. Yet I still refused to believe that I was an alcoholic, at least with my conscious mind. I was determined never again to visit St. Patrick's, which I blamed for my DTs and now for my almost crippled condition. I tried constantly to write, but for the first time in my life it was beyond me. My misery was very great.

On March 27, 1978, I was dining with my children, when I suddenly had to go to the toilet. I could not make it, and fouled my trousers. I have already said how much such an accident distressed me. I telephoned the doctor, and was quite coherent.

I had heard of a place for helping alcoholics—though of course I was, in my opinion, not one—called St. John of God. There something called group therapy was practiced. The term repelled me but I knew I must do something and, as I say, I was determined not to go into St. Patrick's again. Nobody had put the slightest pressure on me this time, neither the doctors nor Marjorie. But Dr. Thomas, my own GP, arranged at once that I be given a private room, with a day and night nurse, in the Hospital of St. John of God, starting the following afternoon.

It was conveniently close to home, a fifteen-minute drive. Marjorie drove me, and we stopped at the pub for what I rather skeptically called my final, large whiskey. I had at last taken my destiny into my own hands, to pass it on to complete strangers.

CHAPTER XX

Endings and Etceteras

First, let me begin this chapter with the concluding list of symptoms given in *Medical Aspects of Alcoholism* under the heading "Chronic Phase." As before, I shall give my own comments in normal print.

1. *Prolonged intoxication.* When I went into St. John of God's, I had been severely intoxicated (which is not the same as being drunk) at least for a couple of months, maybe very much longer, depending on the definition of intoxication.

2. *Marked ethical deterioration.* I have described my sexual and financial ethics in an earlier chapter. These had not deteriorated. Only the sneaking of secret drinks—which in effect is practical lying—might come under this heading.

3. *Impairment of thinking.* Yes, so far as my work was concerned. On the other hand I must have been thinking more clearly in order to put myself in hospital.

4. *Alcoholic psychosis.* I am not quite sure what this means, but do not believe I had become a psychotic.

5. *Drinks below social level.* Odious phrase. I drank, as I had always drunk, at any "social level." Dukes and dustmen are one and the same to me, whether I am drinking or not.

6. *Drinks methylated spirits, after-shave, etc.* Never.

7. *Loss of tolerance.* Yes. Starting some two or three years before going to the hospital and accelerating.

8. *Indefinable fears.* Yes, also quite definable ones, such as fear of becoming a cripple or no longer being able to write. For several years I had in fact been suffering from a deepening depression, of which fear is one part.

9. *Tremors*. No real increase. I had suffered slightly, but only slightly, from the shakes in the morning for many years.

10. *Psychomotor inhibitions*. This means, apparently, a slowing up of mental and physical abilities. I had both. The psychomotor must have been in pretty bad need of a thorough servicing.

And this list of symptoms ends, sternly: "Beyond the prodromal phase, alcoholism is irreversible, and recovery is possible only through total abstinence from alcohol."

I had had a semantic hold-up over the noun "an alcoholic." Was I one or was I not? Nobody seemed able to tell me, nor was the word listed, as a noun, in my *Oxford English Dictionary*. I therefore clung to the fact that I was not an alcoholic, for how could I be something which was semantically non-existent? A drunk, yes, even a drunkard, but all these conversations with doctors, and my wife, all the limited literature I had read was about alcoholics. That Marjorie was a very sick woman in her relationship with alcohol I had seen repeatedly. And I knew that drink was the basic cause of Dylan Thomas's death, and of my sister Mimi's. Yet I was reluctant to describe any of them, let alone myself, as an alcoholic. Words, after all, were my stock in trade. In a life-and-death situation I was hardly willing to use one which apparently had no meaning.

My mind cannot have been quite so addled as perhaps it should have been, for in late March of 1978, sitting alone in my local pub, I suddenly thought: To hell with semantics, I am a very sick man and I need medical help. If they wish to call me "an alcoholic," what difference does it make? Therefore, when I went into St. John of God's and saw the medical director, the celebrated Dr. MacGrath, I had no hesitation in admitting that I was an alcoholic. And I have used the word, invariably with a slight feeling of revulsion, throughout this book. Indeed my sense of outrage at this semantic monstrosity may have been little more than another "rationalization".

In order to be cured of alcoholism three steps are needed. The first is to admit that one needs a cure, that is to say to admit that one is an alcoholic. The second, and easiest, is medical treatment, which falls into two parts since this is a psychophysical disease, the physical being dealt with by the comparatively simple process known as "drying out," the psychological being far more complicated and protracted. The third, for which skilled psychiatric help may be needed, is the realization of the determination to stay off drink, not to surrender to a relapse, which will almost certainly occur if the patient believes that he is in fact cured. He will simply have returned, not to square one, but to square twenty-eight or seventy-three or wherever he found himself when he was dried out *plus* the time that the malady has been progressing while he has not been drinking.

I was dried out in the normal five days, and this time with no withdrawal symptoms, that is to say no DTs. Why this should have been, I do not know. St. John of God's can hardly have possessed any sedative drugs not known also to St. Patrick's. Probably the reason is that I had been generally drinking far less in the days immediately preceding my admittance to St. John of God's than before the other two previous hospitalizations. Also, I arrived there sober, which I had not done at St. Patrick's. Be that as it may, after five days I was up and dressed. I then had an interview with Dr. MacGrath. Did I wish to go home, or did I wish to undergo a course of group therapy lasting twenty-two days? The choice was entirely mine, but he would advise the group therapy. I hesitated, but realized I was being annoyed by the words "group therapy," that I had been dried out before, to no lasting effect, and that I must grasp at this straw, which seemed to me little more than a straw. I made only one condition, that I be given a room to myself. Otherwise I was prepared to submit to all the rules and regulations of "the Unit." Indeed, remembering those happy, distant days as a recruit at Caterham, I rather looked forward to what I was made to understand was pretty strict regimentation.

St. John of God's is a large mental hospital, of which the alcoholics' section is only a small portion and included neither those who had reached the Korsakoff stage nor alcoholic geriatrics. The members of the Unit were, in theory at least, totally confined to one another's company. We had our own sitting room, which we also used for group sessions, and even our own tables in the hospital's communal dining room. We could also use the tea and coffee shop, which was usually either closed or overfilled with people and with smoke. For the first two weeks we were not allowed to leave the hospital grounds, which were large and beautiful. We were, however, permitted visitors in the afternoon. Since my home was only fifteen minutes away, my wife came to see me every day, sometimes accompanied by our daughter, sometimes by Peter, too. Francis was in London. I had no wish to see any other visitors.

The Unit varied in numbers, as some completed their twenty-two days and others joined us after the drying-out process. At first we were all men, but later two women came in. Our numbers varied between about nine and about twelve. The maximum, I was told, was twenty.

The course was supervised by one female and two male nurses, trained in psychiatry and alcoholism. The doctors we hardly saw at all. Dr. Tubridy gave us one lecture a week, on alcoholism. The first two of his that I heard (or rather the same one, twice) he ended briskly with: "No questions!" and left the room. The third, to my surprise, took a question-and-answer form. I say it took me by surprise, for though it was the third time around for me, for newly arrived members of the Unit it was their first. We were lectured three or four times a week by men from Alcoholics Anonymous in addition to hearing, more than once, a long tape by Marty Mann. We were shown films, usually of American or Canadian origin, about certain aspects of alcoholism. Some were highly sensational—I recall one about a female alcoholic—others sentimental, such as the effects on a small child of an alcoholic father. One, by an American priest, was witty and very enlightening. I was glad to see this one twice. Repetition was deliberate and, I think, wise since certain points had to be hammered home in such a way that no one could miss them. But in general we provided our own show, under the supervision of one of the nurses. And this extraordinary intimacy with total strangers, with whom one had usually nothing in common save a desire to be cured of a curse, had one curious, very wholesome, result: lying, even minimizing, became not only pointless but also immediately detectable, detected, and denounced.

There were some ten members of the group when I joined it. When I left I think there were about a dozen members in all. They were of the most diverse provenance, and, quite apart from its real purpose, it was, for me at least, a fascinating lesson in sociology. How else would one get to know, intimately, a detective in the Irish Police Force? They came from all over the English-speaking world, for I believe nothing quite like this unit exists anywhere else. A man from Hong Kong had gone just before I arrived, but there was a priest from Scotland, a world-famous musician from London, an ex-GI who had flown helicopters in Vietnam, a girl telephone operator, an accountant from an American hospital, a farmer from the County Kerry with so broad a brogue that for some days none of us could understand him, the brother of a millionaire speculator, a man who had been much involved in the Belfast fighting. Perhaps the fact that this was in Ireland may have helped to eliminate any form of class distinction. I recall, though, that several of us resented the foul language used by the ex-GI and one other man, and when the women joined us we firmly told them to can it. Curiously perhaps, the one subject we never discussed among ourselves was sex, though we did speak a lot about marital or sexual relationships. This was certainly not modesty on our part, but simply a lack of interest. I regret that our number did not include an alcoholic Freudian psychoanalyst or indeed an alcoholic doctor of any sort.

My GP, David Thomas, came to visit me, as a friend, after I had been in the Unit for three days, to see how I was getting on. I had not really settled down then, and still had doubts as to whether I had done the right thing in undertaking this group therapy. I said to him:

"I have maybe ten or fifteen years of life left to me. I do not want them made miserable by a perpetual craving for a drink, in order to live two or three years longer."

David replied, very seriously: "It would not be a question of ten or fifteen years, but ten or fifteen months."

I believed him, immediately and completely:

"Why on earth didn't you tell me this before?"

"Because if I had—before you made your own choice to come

in here—you would not have believed me and would almost certainly have found yourself a new doctor."

That conversation had as much effect on me as did the Unit. For it was then that I really decided to give up drink, and was able to derive full benefit from the therapy.

Also there was a physiological proof. My legs began rapidly to recover. Again after about three days I was able to walk much better; after a week I was taking long walks around the grounds; after two I abandoned my walking stick.

I regained my faith in God, which I had not realized I had lost. (The Scots priest told me much the same about himself.) And I thought harder, and I think more clearly, than perhaps I had ever done before.

I became conscious of how fortunate I was, and of how much I loved my wife and my children, which meant of course that I loved them more than I had done before, something I should have thought impossible.

I was in fact entering a state of what is coldly called, in the medical books, postalcoholic euphoria. And this came not from giving up drink, which I had previously found at worst a miserable and at best a negligible task. It came from my determination to give up drink by going into the hospital, by learning in the Unit both through talking and through listening, by understanding and believing what David Thomas, surely a master of psychology, had said to me. This is yet a further proof that alcoholism is a psychosomatic malady. My soma was recovering, with my legs, even with my lenseless eyes (for I could see more clearly). It was my psyche that cast aside the depression of years and gave me such happiness.

It did not, however, stop there. When I left the hospital my euphoria increased, my energy seemed boundless, my future utterly assured. I had long known that I was, in rather a mild form, a manic depressive. My mood swings were moderately predictable. For example, the modest satisfaction I derived from satisfactorily finishing a book was usually followed by a modicum of depression. All this had, for years, been in some degree masked by alcohol. Now I was emerging from the very slough of despond into an alcohol-free world, and my euphoria developed into depression's exact counterpart, into hypomania. And for the last week in hospital, and for the first week at home, I did not really fall asleep at all.

This was not an unpleasant insomnia, such as I had very occasionally known and in the past had easily killed with a couple of whiskeys, but a sort of twilight sleep in which my brain was intensely active with plans, good memories, and the formulation of intellectual systems of thought and plans of action, most of which made perfectly good sense when I got up from my bed, fully rested, though I had been glancing at my watch every hour or two all night. A hospital doctor explained to me about "rapid eye movement" sleep, the moments after dropping off and before awakening, and said that it was this. It was, however, a symptom of hypomania.

It was during such a night that I decided I must share my newfound happiness with all my fellow men and women and I outlined the book that I should write. I did this in a couple of days. As a gift of gratitude to Ireland, I wished to be able to say that this book be sponsored by the Government of Ireland. Mr. Lynch, our Taoiseach, or Prime Minister, saw me but said it would be difficult to raise the money I should doubtless need. I told him that I needed none, and next day flew to New York to meet my agent and see my old friend at Doubleday, Ken McCormick, who commissioned the book on the most skeletal outline. Two days later I flew home, but was put on the wrong Concorde. So convincing was I, so sure of myself, that I persuaded Air France in Paris to give me a private plane and fly me to Dublin. I still had had no more than this twilight sleep. (Later, Mr. Lynch's secretary informed me that the Taoiseach could not sponsor this book in any way. I therefore mention my interview with him only as a example of my euphoria at the time.)

This sleeplessness went on for another week or so, till I began to twitch. Much to my annoyance David Thomas forcibly put me back in St. John of God's. I was there for a month and calmed down and began to sleep normally.

When I was at last discharged I immediately went to see Dr. Cooney, who put me on mild anti-depressant pills, for he feared a violent mood swing in the other direction. I then sat down and wrote this book.

In dealing with aids to those victims of alcoholism who would abandon drink, it must be said at once that there are some who need none, while others, perhaps most of those who have been hospitalized, require help for the psychological or the physical aspects of the disease, or for both.

We do not know how many drinkers are sufficiently strong-minded and determined, when they fear the slide into alcoholism, simply to give up drink without even medical aid. The great Dr. Johnson, of the dictionary and of Boswell's biography, discovered at quite an early age that he could not drink. He simply stopped drinking, which did not prevent him from enjoying the company of sots like Boswell or Foote, or of sitting for years on end in the pub called The Cheshire Cheese. Abraham Lincoln's ambivalent attitude toward drink and the temperance fanatics of his day indicates a similar understanding, and the fact that the Lincoln known to history never drank at all might allow one to hazard a guess that he too had tried it while he was still unknown. My wife and I have a friend who got drunk once, when she was a very young girl, and though she mixes in hard-drinking company, she has never drunk again. I know others who have drunk longer and then stopped. It is impossible even to guess at the number of men and women who have done the same. According to Professor Jellinek and general specialist opinion, such cases are likely to have given up in the prodromal stage. It is, however, possible that at least a small number will have gone closer to the abyss.

The man or woman who has been hospitalized will almost invariably need assistance in order to remain sober. To take the physical help first, the progress in drugs has been very real in recent years, though the "wonder drug" that would permit the alcoholic to return to normal drinking has yet to be invented. Since this is a psychosomatic malady, it probably never will be. Meanwhile the discovery of Antabuse has helped millions.

Antabuse is the trade name of a specially purified brand of tetraethyliuram disulfide. The properties of this drug, so far as alcohol is concerned, were discovered in 1948 by two Danish scien-

tists, Jacobsen and Held. They found that if a person who had
been given this drug for some other reason were to take a drink,
he or she would immediately feel extremely ill, with vomiting,
flushing, and a sense of suffocation being the most common
effects. Furthermore, this reaction would take place for several
days after taking the Antabuse, between four and six days usually. It is thus a much more effective version of the old aversion
treatment, as practiced by the late Dr. Dent and others. I am told
that very, very few people who have drunk while taking
Antabuse ever do so again. Not everyone can take it. It is particularly dangerous to those with a weak heart, and doctors will
normally give a patient an Antabuse test before prescribing the
drug. Some doctors distrust it, for it has been the cause of a
few deaths, but far, far fewer than have been caused by alcohol.

The advantage of Antabuse, if taken regularly, is simple. It
prevents the impulsive taking of a drink. It will not hinder the
really determined or, one might say, psychotic drinker, who will
simply stop taking Antabuse for a few days and then get drunk.
But for somebody who has been through the DTs and all the
other miseries of acute alcoholism, a few days is a long time to
think over whether he or she wishes to face all *that* again. And if
he or she has been well informed and *continues to be reminded*
of alcoholic horrors, then Antabuse can be a very real help.

It is also a very real relief to the husband or wife to know that
his or her partner is on Antabuse, maybe to see it taken every
morning, for the man can then go to work without the nagging
fear that his wife might be getting drunk, and vice versa.

Of course drinking alcoholics are notoriously sly. It is quite
possible to pretend to take the pill and then to spit it out: to substitute another pill, say aspirin, in the bottle marked Antabuse:
even to vomit it up. For an alcoholic capable of doing this for
days on end there is, at that time, obviously nothing that can be
done until time and subsequent experience bring about acceptance of the disability.

It can also breed several sorts of resentment. The tactless husband who asks his wife each morning: "Have you taken your Antabuse, dear?" may be heading for trouble. Moreover, certain
people get to resent the drug as such, regarding it as a restriction
to, not an assurance of, their freedom. Here rationalization calls

in the sin of pride: "I am quite capable of looking after myself. I refuse to rely on a drug." This attitude, I regret to say, is encouraged by certain fanatical members of Alcoholics Anonymous, who despise it as "a crutch." Presumably they do not despise a man with a broken leg who uses a crutch.

But there are more and more drugs becoming available which deal with some of the multiple root causes of alcoholism, one of which is most certainly depression. The really expert doctor dealing with alcoholism must be not only a first class psychiatrist and physician but also, in the use of these new and often highly complex drugs, something approaching an expert anesthetist, if he is to keep the precarious reformed alcoholic balanced on the seesaw of manic depression. I do not intend to venture any deeper into this matter, for my ignorance is too great, but I do know that the most remarkable successes are being achieved by a few experts now, and that more can be expected as new and yet better drugs get into more and more highly skilled doctors' hands.

The psychological help is in some ways more complex. It can best be provided by a group of other alcoholics who therefore understand the problems of the disease and would not regard the reformed alcoholic with disdain, even when he has had a relapse. The best known of such groups is Alcoholics Anonymous, founded in America in 1935, but with a long ancestry of similar nature stretching back to the Washingtonians of the early nineteenth century. This is essentially a sort of club, open to all alcoholics, whose members can discuss their problems, past and present, with others in the same or similar predicaments. Many former drunkards do not wish to frequent bars and are made uncomfortable by their old drinking friends. So AA provides them with new friends in a new environment. Some inevitably become fanatics, nor is it unknown for members to turn up drunk. Some are ordered to attend, by wives or by the boss, as in the Dolmetch incident. This is obviously useless. But in general the AA groups offer an immensely useful service, particularly in the United States, where it is reckoned that membership has saved hundreds of thousands, if not millions, from permanent and fatal relapse. Most doctors will advise their alcoholic patients, on leaving hospital, to try AA. It also has a subsidiary called Alanon which informs husbands and wives of the nature of the spouse's disease. If an ex-alcoholic has a slip, he or she can telephone, and a fellow member will come immediately to comfort, look after him or her, and perhaps lead the person in trouble back to sobriety. For details of AA the reader is referred to *Primer on Alcoholism,* by Marty Mann, already mentioned several times in this book. Marty Mann helped introduce AA to Europe, via Ireland, shortly after the Second World War. She is that organization's principal spokeswoman.

More selective, perhaps, are certain groups organized by psychiatrists who are also specialists in alcoholism. I know only one personally, which is Dr. Cooney's "Thursday group" at St. Patrick's Hospital. Twenty or so alcoholics meet almost every Thursday afternoon for an hour to discuss whatever topics may come up concerning alcoholism. Dr. Cooney guides, but does not control, the conversation most skillfully. It is a constant reminder to the alcoholic that he or she is still an alcoholic even though some of those present may not have touched a drink in years, while others may have been dried out last week. The meetings are serious but not solemn, indeed with quite a lot of laughter, a sure proof of a sense of proportion.

My wife has been attending these meetings now for eight years, and would sincerely miss them if they were to cease. As with the members of the Unit, honesty seems automatic. Dishonesty would be immediately detected both by the other members of the group and by Dr. Cooney. Many who attend these Thursday meetings also go to AA meetings, but both Marjorie and I feel that this would be excessive.

To end this autobiographical note, I would say that the combination of Antabuse, Thursday meetings, and Dr. Cooney's skillful prescription of drugs has probably made Marjorie achieve the state of contented sobriety which is the objective of all reformed alcoholics. For myself, and for all others who have suffered or are suffering from this disease, I can only hope that we too may achieve this. If so, the principal credit must go to ourselves, our own intelligence and above all our willpower, which can also be called the help of God.

APPENDIX I

ALCOHOLISM AND THE INDUSTRIAL WORKER

This appendix is extracted from a report to the Minister for Health in the Government of the Republic of Ireland, prepared by the Irish National Council on Alcoholism, after an international conference on alcoholism had been held in Ireland in 1971. It is here published with permission of the National Council.

1. ATTITUDES OF MANAGEMENT AND UNIONS

There is undoubtedly serious economic loss to the nation as a result of undisclosed and untreated alcoholism and excessive drinking at all levels in industry. On the one hand there is a general reluctance by management to admit the existence of a problem; the trade union movement, on the other hand, accepts that the problem exists, and is increasing. At the All-Ireland Conference on "Alcoholism at Work," held in Newry in 1971, the trade unions were obviously more aware of the serious effects of alcoholism in industry than were management representatives. The concern of the trade union movement is demonstrated in the following motion which was proposed by the Irish Union of Distributive Workers and Clerks, and adopted by the Annual Delegate Meeting of the Irish Congress of Trade Unions, in July 1972:

"Recognizing that alcoholism in Ireland is an increasing social problem, that it is a serious cause of loss of man-hours in industry, and a potential source of industrial strife, that Conference would instruct the Executive Committee to enter into early negotiations with the F.U.E. with a view to establishing agreed principles or procedures in the treatment of workers who are victims."

a. The economic cost which can be attributed directly to the alcoholic may be listed under a number of headings:

   1. absenteeism, particularly following weekends and holidays
   2. unusually high accident-proneness

3. abnormal and repetitive minor ailment occurrences
4. loss of production due to faulty workmanship
5. disproportionately high waste of raw material
6. faulty decisions at executive level
7. cost of training replacements for persons dismissed for alcoholism or heavy drinking.

In addition, there is the undoubted fact that alcoholics and excessive drinkers frequently report for work apparently in reasonable physical and mental shape, whereas they are often incapable of doing a proper day's work. Initially, at least, these workers are "covered up" by their fellow workers, who themselves, in attempting to perform more than a normal amount of work, often reduce their own efficiency.

b. The eventual dismissal of the alcoholic or problem-drinking employee by management leads ultimately to a deterioration in labor-management relations, and is a potential source of industrial strife.

2. LACK OF DATA ON THE EXTENT OF THE PROBLEM

Because of the general reluctance of Irish management to admit to the existence of a problem, and the lack of any known survey carried out by management to determine the existence and extent of the problem, there is little hard information available in relation to its effect on Irish industry. There is, however, no reason to think that industry in Ireland is different in this respect from other countries where such studies have been made. Moreover, there are certain pointers applicable to the Irish scene which would indicate the existence of a problem:

a. In 1970 there was considerable public concern that over one million workdays were lost through industrial strife. The same concern is not evident in relation to the very much greater loss of man days through illness. Mr. R. Roberts, General Secretary of the Irish Congress of Trade Unions, disclosed at a symposium held in 1971 that some 16 million workdays were lost in 1969 because of absenteeism through illness. The size of the threat posed by absenteeism to Ireland's economic growth is highlighted in an article in *Business and Finance* of November 18, 1971. The article refers specifically to the appalling absence rates disclosed by a number of firms which maintained records in response to a request from a research team from the Institute of Public Administration. In view of the evidence already presented, it may be assumed that a significant number of days so lost could be attributed directly or indirectly to alcoholism and excessive drinking.

b. Dr. Sean O'Quigley completed a very comprehensive study of absence from work attributed to illness.* Dr. O'Quigley pointed to the annually increasing amount of time lost between 1961 and 1967 due to absence from work attributed to illness. These figures, based on the Social Welfare Disability benefits paid on claims, do not record, however, the full extent of such absence. Periods of illness of three days or less were not included. Dr. O'Quigley did not attempt to estimate how much of this absence might be attributed directly or indirectly to alcoholism or problem drinking—clearly an impossible task in the light of the limited amount of specific information on the subject. In the context of alcoholism, he did have this to say: "There is one type of patient we find difficult to rehabilitate—the alcoholic. In these cases I think that the rescue rate would be higher if the general practitioner concerned conferred with the Industrial Doctor sooner. I have never seen a doctor's certificate which stated that the patient could not attend work because he was an alcoholic. I think that perhaps in being over-protective towards those patients, we run the risk of making the root cause more deep-seated."

c. Many studies on alcoholism in American industry have been made, and the loss estimates vary from 4 to 10 billion dollars per year. Applying this proportionately to Ireland, and assuming the rate of loss to be only 10 per cent of the largest American figure, Irish industry could lose approximately 6 million pounds annually.

3. EXPERIENCE IN THE UNITED STATES OF AMERICA

A number of progressive American firms have introduced alcoholism programs which are designed to assist and motivate the problem-drinking employee to treatment and recovery. The most generally accepted finding is that investment in such a program provides a return of from four to ten dollars for every dollar invested. This

* *Irish Journal of Medical Science*, "Absence from Work Attributed to Illness", vol. 3, no. 11, November 1970, p. 513, vol. 3, no. 12, December 1970, p. 563.

profitability is achieved by reduction of absenteeism, on-the-job accidents, waste material, and the time and expense of training replacements for those who ordinarily might have been dismissed because of their problem drinking.

a. The U. S. Postal Service, in a study undertaken of the Boston Post Office system in 1971, discovered that a saving of 4.07 dollars had been made for every dollar invested in its alcoholism program. The New York Transit Authority calculates that it saves 1 million dollars yearly in sick pay alone.

b. The absentee rate of employees of Consolidated Edison was reduced by 66 per cent, and that of Allis Chalmers from 8 to 3 per cent following the introduction of alcoholism programs.

c. The recovery rate is closely related to the stage of alcoholism reached before discovery and presentation for treatment. In the case of late discovery, recovery is low. On the other hand, where discovery is made in the early stages, the following companies report a success rate as below for their problem drinkers, which permitted their retention in employment:

The Kemper Institute	75 per cent
The Norton Company	92 per cent
Allis Chalmers	87 per cent
Cyanamid Company	86 per cent
Consolidated Edison	76 per cent
Du Pont	66 per cent

d. Allis Chalmers reported a reduction in its scrap metal to a negligible amount, and an improvement in its safety record.

e. It is American experience that joint labor/management alcoholism programs have in some cases replaced what was once an industrial battleground. Summary dismissal for alcoholism has grown less common, and as a result, companies with alcoholism programs now receive union cooperation more often than not.

4. MANAGEMENT

Alcoholism and excessive drinking are not confined to the factory floor. They exist at management level, where the effect is often more costly to the efficiency of the industry concerned.

5. THE PUBLIC SERVICE

Alcoholism and excessive drinking are not confined to industry—they exist in the public service and in other professions, and in State organizations, including the defense forces and the Irish Police. Profitability in the same sense as in industry is not affected, but there can be a significant loss of efficiency through absenteeism, poor job performance, minor and major illnesses, and faulty decisions.

6. PREVENTION

Alcoholics can be reached more effectively through their jobs than through any other aspect of their lives. Thus management and employers are in a unique position to assist in prevention. It is clearly in the best interests of the nation that programs on alcoholism be introduced in these areas. The State, which is the largest single employer in the country, should set the lead, as an example both to State-sponsored bodies and the private sector by the introduction of an alcoholism program for its employees.

7. POLICY

The State should also encourage industry, by financial incentives as necessary, to develop such programs. Such programs might incorporate a policy statement which would include, *inter alia,* the following concepts:
a. the regard for the employee as an industrial human being as well as a worker
b. that alcoholism is an illness and should be treated as such
c. that the majority of problem drinkers can be helped to recovery, and the employer should offer appropriate assistance
d. that the decision to undergo treatment is the responsibility of the employee, and no employee should be forced to accept assistance
e. that it is in the interest of the problem-drinking employee and the employer that the problem be identified and treated while in the early or middle stages if possible
f. that the employer's concern for individual drinking practices begins ONLY when they result in unsatisfactory job performance

g. that the completely confidential handling of problem-drinking situations is essential

h. that the object of this policy is to retain valued employees who are developing a drinking problem, by helping them to recognize, treat, and arrest its further advance before they become unemployable and broken in health.

APPENDIX II

ALCOHOLISM AND ROAD ACCIDENTS

This report was first published by the *Journal of the Irish Medical Association*, vol. 66, no. II, June 9, 1973, and is republished here with their permission and with that of the two authors.* It must be stressed that the report deals with alcoholics, not merely with drunken drivers, that is to say, with only a small percentage of accidents caused in whole or in part by drunkenness.

The relationship between alcohol consumption and road accidents has been the subject of intensive study in recent years. Most research efforts have concentrated upon the relationship between various levels of alcohol in the blood of the driver and the resultant impairment of his driving skills (Holcomb, 1938; McCarroll and Haddon; Haddon and Bradess, 1959; Selzer and Weiss, 1966; Campbell, 1966; Borkenstein et al, 1964).

Less attention has been paid to the contribution made by the alcoholic to the steadily increasing accident rate on the roads. This study was undertaken to investigate the driving histories of a group of alcoholic car drivers in order to answer two main questions: *Firstly,* do alcoholic car drivers accumulate more traffic accidents and violations in their driving careers than non-alcoholic drivers? and *secondly,* at what stage in the development of his alcoholic problem do those accidents and violations involving alcohol occur? Several studies such as this have been undertaken elsewhere, but little is known of the Irish situation, no research of this type having been conducted before.

METHOD

100 male alcoholic car drivers, each with a history of driving for at least two years and an average mileage of at least 3,000 miles per year, were selected according to the age groups in Table I. From

---

* Anthony W. Clare, M.B., M.R.C.I.I., M. Phil. (Lond.) The Maudsley Hospital, Denmark Hill, London. John G. Cooney, M.B., M.R.C. Psych., D.P.M., DPh, D.Chl., St. Patrick's Hospital, Dublin.

March 17, 1969, each alcoholic admitted to St. Patrick's Hospital, and meeting the above requirements, was included in the study. The proportion of drivers in each age group was decided upon after an analysis of the previous year's admissions of male alcoholics to the hospital. The World Health Organization (1952) definition of an alcoholic* was employed for the purpose of this study. A control group of 100 drivers, matched for age, sex and meeting the minimum requirements for driving experience and mileage, was drawn from the outpatient practice of 10 general practitioners. 5 of these practised in the Dublin area and 5 in other areas around the country, a ratio roughly reflecting the ratio of Dublin to non-Dublin alcoholic patients admitted to St. Patrick's Hospital in 1968. Due to illness on the part of one of the non-Dublin general practitioners, and a delay in obtaining information from one of the Dublin practitioners, the control group was unavoidably reduced to 80 drivers.

The alcoholic and control groups were questioned regarding occupation, number of years driving, average yearly mileage, history of prosecutions and/or accidents. Prosecutions included all traffic violations, save those related to parking offences. Accidents were classified as minor, moderate and major accidents. A minor traffic accident was one in which no personal injury was sustained and car damage did not exceed £100. A moderate accident was one in which personal injuries of a minor nature, such as cuts, bruises, minor fractures necessitating treatment or hospital attention of up to 24 hours duration, were sustained, or where car damage exceeded £100, or where the car or cars were extensively damaged or written off. A major accident was one in which severe personal injuries were sustained, or a person or persons killed. Identical questionnaires were applied to each group, the method having been carefully standardized beforehand with doctors involved in the study. The alcoholic group was also questioned regarding the approximate time of onset of such alcoholic symptoms as blackouts, gulping drinks, loss of control, regular morning drinking, withdrawal symptoms including fits, shakes and delirium tremens. In addition, information was sought from this group in respect of their hospitalizations for conditions often relating to, or associated with

---

* . . . "Alcoholics are those excessive drinkers whose dependence on alcohol has attained such a degree that they show a noticeable mental disturbance or an interference with their mental and bodily health, their interpersonal relations and their smooth social and economic functioning; or who show the prodromal signs of such developments."

alcoholism, i.e., gastric symptoms, liver disease, cardiac disease and pneumonia. It was stressed to all the participants that the study was of purely medical interest and had no legal implications.

RESULTS

The alcoholic and control groups did not differ to any statistically significant degree with respect to age, driving experience and mileage driven. See Table I.

Table I General Data

Age	No. in Alcoholic Sample	No. in Control Group
21–30 years	10	8
31–40 years	40	32
41–50 years	30	24
51–60 years	20	16
Total	100	80

Table II

Prosecutions	Alcoholic Group—100	Control Group—80
Speeding	19	3
Dangerous Driving	10	2
Drunken Driving	19	—
Drunken and Dangerous Driving	9	—
Failing to Stop	1	1
Defective Vehicle	—	2
Overtaking	1	—
Crossing White Line	2	—
Total	61	13

PROSECUTIONS

Of the 61 prosecutions sustained by the alcoholic sample, 28 (45.9%) involved drunken or drunken and dangerous driving. None of the prosecutions sustained by the control group involved alcohol and no comparative figure exists for the association of heavy drinking and accidents in the control group.

Table III

Accidents	Alcoholic Group—100	Control Group—80
Minor	90	45
Moderate	65	17
Major	8 (5 non-fatal) (3 fatal)	4 (non-fatal)
Total	163	66

ACCIDENTS

The alcoholic group of 100 patients had accumulated a total of 163 accidents, 90 minor, 65 moderate and 8 major, as compared with the 66 accidents, 45 minor, 17 moderate and 4 major, of the control group of 80 patients.

In 72 (44%) of the 163 accidents detailed by the alcoholic sample, the alcoholic driver admitted to drinking heavily around the time of the accident.

ALCOHOLISM

Details regarding the incidence and age of onset of a variety of symptoms characteristic of an alcoholic's drinking pattern are set out in Table IV. A blackout was defined, after Keller, as "amnesia for the events of any part of a drinking episode, without loss of consciousness" (Keller and Seeley, 1958). Loss of control was judged to exist when the patient gave a history of being unable to drink socially (have a few drinks, and then stop), or when one or two drinks triggered a severe drinking bout. In Table IV, the age at which the first traffic accidents or prosecutions in which alcohol was implicated is included, as is the age at which the alcoholic was first hospitalized for his alcoholism.

Table IV Onset of Alcoholic Manifestations among 100 Alcoholics

Manifestation	Present (%)	Mean Age at Onset
Gulping Drinks	76	31
Alcoholic Amnesiae (Blackouts)	87	32
First Accident or Violation involving Alcohol	49	32

Loss of Control	87	33
Regular Morning Drinking	69	34
Withdrawal and 'Shakes'	54	36
First Admission for Alcoholism	100	38
First Accident or Violation	84	31

Table V Alcoholic patients treated in General Hospital for physical symptoms related to Alcoholism

No. of Patients	Condition
14	Peptic Ulcer
5	'Gastritis'
6	Liver disease
5	Pneumonia
3	Tuberculosis
2	Withdrawal symptoms
2	Cardiac disease
___	
37	

HOSPITALIZATIONS

37 of the 100 alcoholics had been treated in general hospitals for physical symptoms related to, or associated with their alcoholism. 19 of these were treated for gastric symptoms and in 14 of the 19, peptic ulcer was diagnosed. 5 of the 14 had surgery. 6 patients were treated for liver disease, 5 for pneumonia, 3 for tuberculosis, 2 for withdrawal symptoms and 2 for cardiac symptoms. One of the alcoholic patients treated for gastric symptoms was later treated for liver disease, hence there were thirty-eight hospital admissions shared by 37 alcoholics.

DISCUSSION

The study confirmed that the alcoholic driver in Ireland has a significantly greater number of accidents and violations in his driving record than a matched control group (p>0.01) Alcoholics had approximately four times as many prosecutions and twice as many accidents as control drivers. This result is remarkably similar to that obtained by Schmidt and Smart in Canada (1959, 1962), Selzer and Weiss in the U.S. (1966) and Bjerver et al. in Sweden (1955). In 8 of the 28 prosecutions involving alcohol the charges were withdrawn for lack of evidence, although in each case the driver in retrospect believed himself to have been quite drunk. In one such case the alcoholic passed the medical test and the prosecution for drunken driving was withdrawn; although he afterwards stated that at the time he was convinced he was drunk when he passed the Garda doctor's test. Within the following year he was involved in another accident. It would appear at the time of his arrest for drunken driving, this man showed many of the major signs of alcoholism.

Of the 72 accidents where alcohol was stated by the alcoholic to have played a major part, only 19 reached the courts. This supports Glatt's view (1960) that the vast majority of road accidents involving misuse of alcohol do not appear in the official road accident statistics or in the criminal statistics. In 5 of the 19 cases which resulted in prosecution the alcoholic drivers were fined, the fines varying from £2 to £20. In one of these cases the alcoholic drove into a squad car. Though he himself was convinced he was drunk, he passed the Garda doctor's test. The patient was clinically recognizable as an alcoholic at the time and went on to have another accident within the year. In another case, the alcoholic driver ran into a hitch hiker on the road and killed him. The driver admitted he had been drinking—"only a small whiskey and half a pint of stout" —but agreed that he may have had more in the preceding few hours. The medical history strongly suggests that he had been an alcoholic for the previous nine years, at least. He was fined £20 on this occasion. Another year passed before he was hospitalized for his alcoholism and brought to the realization of his drinking problem. A third driver admitted to drinking 13 pints of beer before he wrecked his own car and another, in a head-on collision. He was fined £14. Within 6 months he was involved in a similar collision and this time was fined £25 and had his licence suspended for one year. Six cases resulted in both fines and licence suspensions. In one of these, a head-on collision, the alcoholic driver admitted to an intake of 10 whiskies in the two hours prior to the accidents, two of them, he claimed, occurring in the course of blackouts.

In four accidents where prosecutory proceedings were initiated, the charges were later withdrawn for lack of evidence; at the time of the survey a charge was pending against one of the alcoholic drivers. Another alcoholic driver received a three months suspended sentence around this time also. Another charge following on a head-on collision in which the other driver was killed, resulted in the alcoholic driver being jailed for one year and being disqualified from driving for life. In only one of the 19 prosecutions was the other driver, i.e., the non-alcoholic driver, prosecuted and fined. Thus, only 71 per cent of the charges involving alcohol and 77 per cent of the small number of accidents that did go to the courts resulted in convictions, similar, if slightly higher figures than the official ratio of convictions to prosecutions in the field of road traffic offences (Gar. Pub. O, 1963).

PATTERN OF ACCIDENTS IN ALCOHOLIC AND CONTROL GROUPS

It was not possible to ascertain the part played by alcohol in the accidents sustained by the control group. The pattern of accidents in each group was, however, worthy of note. (Table VI) Of the 163 accidents in the alcohol group, 73 were single vehicle accidents, 69 involved another moving vehicle or vehicles, 11 involved another car which was parked or stopped, 4 involved cyclists, 3 involved

Table VI

Accident Type	Alcoholic Group—100 (With % of total in parentheses)	Control Group—80
Single Vehicle Accidents	73(44.7%)	18(27.3%)
Multiple Vehicle Accidents	69(42.3%)	36(54.6%)
Accident involving parked or stopped Vehicle	11(6.9%)	9(13.6%)
Accident involving Motor Cyclists	3(1.9%)	—
Accident involving Cyclists	4(2.3%)	2(3%)
Accident involving Pedestrians	3(1.9%)	1(1.5%)
Total	163	66

motor cyclists and 3 involved pedestrians. Of the 90 accidents involving other vehicles, both moving and stationary, cyclists, motor cyclists and pedestrians, the alcoholic driver accepted liability, or was prosecuted in 57, the other driver accepted liability, or was prosecuted in 25, and in 8 responsibility for the accident was shared. Thus, in 130 of the 163 accidents (79.7%) the alcoholic driver was primarily responsible. In the control group there were 18 single vehicle accidents, 36 accidents involving one or more moving vehicles, 9 accidents involving a parked or stopped car, 2 collisions with cyclists and one accident involving a pedestrian. Of the 48 accidents involving other vehicles, moving or stopped, cyclists and pedestrians, the control driver was prosecuted or accepted liability in 19, the other driver or pedestrian accepted responsibility, or was prosecuted in 17, and responsibility was shared or disputed in 12. Thus, in 37 of the 66 control accidents (56%) the control driver was primarily responsible for the accident.

ALCOHOLISM AND ROAD ACCIDENTS

This study highlights the typical pattern of development of alcoholism. The average alcoholic shows the first signs of trouble in his early thirties with appearance of gulping drinks, loss of control in his drinking and blackouts. By his mid-thirties, well-established signs of physical dependence e.g. regular morning drinking and withdrawal symptoms are seen, and by his late thirties he enters hospital for the first time. But what this paper also shows is that while the average alcoholic receives formal treatment when he is 38 or more he has his first accident resultant on his drinking at least 6 years before this, and relatively early in the development of his alcoholic condition. This pattern is quite similar to that shown by Glatt (1959) who constructed such a pattern from replies to Jellinek's questionnaires.

Of the 49 alcoholic drivers with a history of first accident or violation involving alcohol, 36 were recognizable clinically at the time of their accidents or violations as alcoholics while the remaining 13 showed premonitory signs of a developing alcohol problem. Schmidt et al. in their Toronto study demonstrated that 28 per cent of all drivers convicted of impaired or drunken driving were alcoholic in the clinical sense (Schmidt and Smart, 1962). Selzer and Weiss (1966) in a study of 72 drivers responsible for fatal accidents in Ann Arbor, Michigan, found that 40 per cent were established alcoholics, while a further 10 per cent were pre-alcoholic and in another study Selzer et al. (1963) claimed that in almost three-quarters of those convicted of drunken driving, a serious problem with alcohol was found. These findings have prompted some workers, including Campbell (1967), to recommend closer liaison between the courts and the medical authorities, in order that the alcoholic driver can be identified as early in his driving career as possible, so that he can be restrained, treated and rehabilitated.

Blackouts. It is worth noting that a high proportion of the alcoholic sample, 87 per cent, gave a history of blackouts. In most of these patients alcoholic amnesia was one of the first signs of a developing alcoholic problem.

ALCOHOLISM IN GENERAL HOSPITALS

This study supports the views of other workers (Nolan, 1965; Green, 1965; Pearson, 1962) that many alcoholics are admitted to general hospitals for evaluation of symptoms related to or associated with their alcoholism but receive little in the way of systematic treatment for their pathological drinking. 38 patients, just over one-third of the total alcoholic sample, had been hospitalized for conditions associated with excessive drinking. 23 of the 38—Table VII—had been admitted to general hospitals after the onset of their alcoholism and before their first admission to an inpatient unit for specific treatment for their drinking; 5 hospitalizations were for pneumonia, 3 for liver conditions, 2 for tuberculosis, 2 for withdrawal symptoms, 2 for cardiac symptoms and 9 for gastric complaints. At the time of admission, all 23 patients manifested the clinical signs of alcoholism yet only 2 were encouraged to seek treatment for their alcoholism. On average the admission for a physical condition occurred about 6 years after the onset of the drinking problem and a further four years elapsed before the patient was first admitted for formal treatment of his drinking problem.

Table VII Alcoholic Patients Treated in General Hospitals After Onset of Alcoholism

No. of Patients	Condition
5	Pneumonia
3	Liver Disease
2	Tuberculosis
2	Withdrawal Symptoms
9	'Gastric' Symptoms
2	Cardiac Disease
23	

Two of the 9 patients admitted for gastric symptoms were treated surgically. In the first case it was 5 years, and in the second 16, before the patient received formal treatment for his alcoholism—although at the time of the operation it would appear that each patient was clinically recognizable as an alcoholic. It is pertinent to note that both these patients were involved in serious road accidents during the period between their admissions for their operations and their first admissions for formal treatment of their drinking, moreover in each case, the patient attributed the accident to his excessive intake of alcohol.

2 patients were treated for cardiac symptoms after a drinking problem had developed. One was diagnosed as a coronary. According to this patient, however, he was advised merely to avoid spirits. Four years were to elapse before he received treatment for his alcoholism.

Thus over 20 per cent of the alcoholic sample appeared before medical specialists for conditions related to or associated with alcoholism on average some 6 years after the onset of a drinking problem. Yet for the average alcoholic so presenting this was not the moment for his drinking problem to be identified. On average another four years were to elapse before his drinking problem was officially recognized and treated. These figures reinforce the findings of Nolan (1965) who considered 13.8 per cent of 900 consecutive admissions to a community hospital to have a significant problem with alcohol and who believed that such a figure was probably a conservative estimate. Green (1965) studied admissions to a public hospital and claimed, again as a conservative estimate, that one in every five males and one in every twenty-seven females were established alcoholics. Pearson (1962) found that only 3 of 29 alcoholics in a general medical ward were recognized to have such a problem by their attending physicians. The unavoidable conclusion in our study is that alcoholics who present in general hospitals are very often not diagnosed even when they present with conditions which are well recognized as being associated with excessive consumption of alcohol.

CONCLUSIONS

This study of the driving histories of 100 male alcoholics and 80 control drivers confirms that alcoholics accumulate a significantly increased incidence of road accidents and prosecutions. A sizeable proportion, 45.9 per cent, of the prosecutions sustained by the alcoholic group involved drunken or drunken and dangerous driving. In 44 per cent of the accidents alcohol played a significant part. These figures, established by questioning the alcoholic himself, are remarkably similar to findings in other studies, where, in addition to obtaining information from the alcoholic himself, recourse was had to legal records, casualty details and post-mortem studies. It would appear, therefore, that retrospective falsification was of little significance in the results obtained.

It was clear from our survey that the official figures for drunken driving and accidents involving alcohol are not sufficiently detailed to allow a clear perspective to be obtained. Of the accidents and violations that do reach the courts almost 25 per cent were withdrawn or dismissed for lack of evidence. It should be pointed out, however, that at the time of this study, breathalyser tests and blood alcohol level estimates were not employed. It would appear that the introduction of these tests will radically alter the picture (B.M.J. 1971).

This study confirms the belief that an accident or prosecution involving alcohol occurs early in an alcoholic's history. Thus, the eliciting of information regarding such an accident or prosecution in the patient's history can be helpful in establishing the diagnosis of alcoholism and should, these days, be sought for as routinely as the other classical signs and symptoms of alcoholism.

23 of the alcoholic patients were recognizably suffering from alcoholism at the time that they presented at general hospitals for the treatment of physical conditions related to, or associated with, alcoholism. Many of these patients, however, did not receive formal treatment for their alcoholism for over four years.

It would therefore seem that alcoholics, during their progressive course, present at general hospitals for associated and related conditions and at the courts for accidents and prosecutions in which drink is involved. The diagnosis is still being missed because those who come into contact with the patient, that is, doctors, nurses, social workers, police and legal officials are not alert to the existence of alcoholism in the patient. One reason for the alcoholic condition being overlooked may be the erroneous belief of so many people that the average alcoholic conforms to the stereotype of the 'skid row' down and out. The fact that the majority of alcoholics for most of their drinking career are as well dressed and as healthy looking as any comparable section of the community is often not realized.

Until this situation is altered, until medical and surgical consultants show a greater awareness of the nature and extent of alcoholism in general hospital admissions, then alcoholism will continue to be missed in the early stages before irrevocable and irreparable damage follows. Again, in those accidents where alcohol is involved, a more intensive effort must be made to identify the alcoholic driver by the gardai, police surgeons, general practitioners and casualty officers who come in contact with him. Alcoholics should receive treatment and be rehabilitated before being allowed to drive again. It should be possible for judges to bring this about by directing that alcoholic drivers who come within their jurisdiction must undergo treatment. If this were done, a significant decrease in the number of road accidents would be brought about.

In this regard it is heartening to be able to report that, following the presentation at the Dun Laoire Conference on Alcoholism in September 1971, District Justice Michael McGrath was moved to set about the initiation of an Alcohol Education Programme in the Midlands. This Programme, which came into being in the summer of 1972, was devised, implemented and coordinated by the Court Welfare Officer, (Department of Justice), with the cooperation of the Road Safety Officer of the Department of Local Government, the Midland and Western Health Board Psychiatric Services, and others.

It is to be hoped that the results of this innovation will parallel those of the Phoenix, Arizona D.W.I. (DRINKING WHILE DRIVING) Programme, which appears to have had a considerable impact on what is now a major health hazard in our motorized Western world.

ACKNOWLEDGMENTS

We wish to record our gratitude to the practitioners who cooperated so wholeheartedly with us. Our thanks are also due to Mr. James McGilvray, formerly of the Department of Economics, Trinity College, Dublin, for his helpful advice regarding the setting out and standardization of the Survey. We are particularly indebted to Professors J. N. P. Moore and Peter G. Beckett, for their comments and advice on the Project and Paper.

REFERENCES

Borkenstein, R.F., Crowther, R.F., Shumate, R.P., Ziel, W.B. and Zylman, R. (Dale, A. ed.). The role of the drinking driver in traffic accidents. Bloomington, Ind. Indiana University. Dept. of Police Administration 1964.

B.M.J., 2nd October 1971.

Bjerver, K.B. Proceedings of 2nd International Conference. Alcohol and Road Traffic. Toronto. Alcohol Research Foundation 1955.

Campbell, H.E. Traffic deaths go up again. *J. Amer. Med. Ass.* 201 No. 11. 861-864.

Campbell, H.E. The role of alcohol in fatal traffic "accidents" and measures needed to solve the problem. *Mich. Med.* 63, 699-703

Feeney, F.E., Mindlin, D.F., Minear, V.H. and Short, E.E. The challenge of the skid row alcoholic. A Social, psychological and psychiatric comparison of chronically jailed alcoholics and co-operative alcoholic clinic patients. (1955) *Quar. J. Stud. Alcohol* 16, 645-667.

Glatt, M.M. Alcoholism in "impaired" and drunken driving. (1960) *Lancet* 1, 161-163.

Government Commission on "driving while under the Influence of Drink or Drugs". Government Publication Office. Dublin 1963.

Glatt, M.M. An Alcoholic Unit in a Mental Hospital (1959) *Lancet* 11, 397-398.

Goodwin, D.W., Crane, J.B. and Guze, G.B. Alcoholic "Blackouts". A review and clinical study of 100 alcoholics. *Amer. J. Psychiat.* 126, 2, 191-219.

Green, J.R. The incidence of alcoholism in patients admitted to medical wards of a public hospital (1965) *Med. J. of Australia*, 485-486.

Holcomb, R.L. Alcohol in relation to traffic accidents. (1938) *J. Amer. Med. Ass.* 111, 1076-1085.

Haddon, W. Jnr. and Bradess, V.A. Alcohol in the single vehicle fatal accident; experience of Westchester County, New York. (1959) *J. Amer. Med. Ass.* 169, 1587-1593.

Jellinek, E.M. Phases in the Drinking Histories of Alcoholics. Analysis of a Survey conducted by the official organ of A.A. (1946) *Quart. J. Stud. Alc.* 7, 1-88.

Jellinek, E.M. The Phases of Alcohol Addiction. (1952) *Quart. J. Stud. Alc.* 13, 673-684.

Keller, M. and Seeley, J.R. The alcohol language. Toronto. Univ. of Toronto Press 1958.

McCarroll, J.R. and Haddon, W. Jnr. A controlled study of fatal automobile accidents in New York City. (1962) *J. Chronic Dis.* 15, 811-826.

Nolan, J.P. Alcohol as a factor in the illness of University Service Patients. (1965) *Amer. J. of Med. Science*, 37-44.

Pearson, W.S. (1962) *North Carolina Med. Journal*, 23, 6.

Selzer, M.L. and Weiss, S. Alcoholism and traffic fatalities; study in futility. (1966) *Amer. J. Psychiat.*, 122, 762-767.

Schmidt, W.S. and Smart, R.G. Alcohol Drinking and Traffic Accidents. (1959) *Quart. J. Study Alc.* 20, 631-644.

Schmidt, W.S. and Smart, R.G. Alcohol and Road Traffic. Proceedings of 3rd International Conference. P. 90. London 1962.

Selzer, M.L., Payne, C.E., Gifford, J.D. and Kelly, W.L., Alcoholism, Mental Illness and "Drinking Driver". (1963) *Amer. J. Psychiat.*, 120, 326-331.

World Health Organization. Expert Committee on Mental Health 1952. Alcoholic Subcommittee. 2nd Report. WHO Technical Series No. 48.

Williams, J.H. Characteristics of an Alcoholic Sample. Avon Park, Florida. Florida Alcoholic Rehabilitation Programme. 1964.

APPENDIX III

INTERNATIONAL PER CAPITA CONSUMPTION OF ALCOHOL, 1976

ISSUED BY THE IRISH NATIONAL COUNCIL ON ALCOHOLISM

Country	Litres of absolute alcohol, all beverages	Litres of absolute alcohol, all spirits	Litres of bulk beer	Litres of bulk wine
1. France	16.5	2.5	48.66	101.3
2. Portugal	14.1	1.0	27.7	97.8
3. Spain	14.0	3.1	47.9	71.0
4. Luxembourg	13.4	4.1	130.0	45.3
5. Italy	12.7	2.0	13.9	99.7
6. West Germany	12.5	2.83	150.9	23.6
7. Austria	11.2	1.7	102.0	36.3
8. Argentina	10.7	?	10.4	84.8
9. Hungary	10.7	4.1	77.0	34.0
10. Switzerland	10.3	1.8	71.1	43.5
11. Belgium	10.2	1.95	145.0	15.7
12. Australia	9.6	1.3	139.9	11.2
13. New Zealand	9.3	1.7	131.0	8.8
14. Denmark	9.2	1.90	118.68	12.53
15. Czechoslovakia	9.2	3.0	139.4	16.5
16. Yugoslavia	8.9	3.5	39.0	28.6
17. Canada	8.6	3.24	84.7	7.0
18. Netherlands	8.3	2.49	83.8	11.34
19. East Germany	8.3	3.6	124.5	7.0
20. Poland	8.2	5.4	34.9	8.5
21. United States of America	8.1	3.12	82.5	6.64
22. Rumania	8.1	2.4	35.0	30.0
23. Republic of Ireland	7.0	1.98*	123.0	3.09

* Owing to a difference in the manner of measurement, in fact the consumption per capita of beers is slightly higher in the United Kingdom than in the Republic of Ireland, and the consumption of litres of absolute alcohol, all beverages, approximately the same.

Appendix

Country	Litres of absolute alcohol, all beverages	Litres of absolute alcohol, all spirits	Litres of bulk beer	Litres of bulk wine
24. United Kingdom	6.8	1.66	118.9	5.64
25. Bulgaria	6.7	2.0	46.0	20.0
26. Finland	6.4	3.0	54.6	8.5
27. Chile	6.2	?	10.1	47.84
28. USSR	6.1	3.3	23.3	13.4
29. Sweden	5.9	3.08	59.1	8.47
30. Greece	5.5	?	15.0	39.8
31. Japan	5.2	1.4	32.4	0.27
32. Israel	1.8	.9	10.0	3.61

APPENDIX IV

ALCOHOL AND YOUR UNBORN BABY

Issued by the National Institute on Alcohol Abuse and Alcoholism, Department of Health, Education, and Welfare, 5600 FISHER'S LANE, ROCKVILLE, MARYLAND 20854. It is dated 1978 and reproduced here with their permission.

For most women, pregnancy is a time of intense, often mixed feelings. The good feelings can be very good; anticipation, pride, excitement, a sense of fulfillment. But because having a baby is such an important event in one's life, it is also natural to experience some doubts and fears along with the "highs." Even in the most wanted of pregnancies, many women wonder: Can I handle the responsibility of another person for the next eighteen years? Can I afford this baby? Will it be a difficult birth? And, perhaps most frightening of all, will I have a normal, healthy child? Or will it be born with some kind of physical or mental problem?

Few women have not worried about the last possibility at some point during their pregnancy. But what many women don't know is that there are a number of things they can do during pregnancy to increase the chances of delivering a healthy baby. Regular prenatal check-ups and a nutritious diet are important. But an expectant mother also should be extremely careful about the kinds and amounts of drugs she takes. In addition to many illegal drugs, several legal drugs are known to cause birth defects when taken during pregnancy. Recently, our most popular legal drug has been added to the list: ALCOHOL.

ALCOHOL: A POWERFUL DRUG

Alcohol is so taken for granted in our society that most of us don't even think of it as a drug. Yet whenever we have wine with a meal, a gin and tonic at a party, or a beer with the late movie, we are consuming a central nervous system depressant that affects nearly every organ in our bodies. Alcohol abuse over a period of time can contribute to a number of serious disorders, including muscle and heart disease, malnutrition, digestive problems and liver cirrhosis. It should not be surprising that this powerful addictive drug, when abused during pregnancy, can also affect the delicate system of the unborn baby.

EFFECTS OF HEAVY DRINKING ON THE UNBORN BABY

In the last several years, researchers have conducted a number of studies on infants born to women who drank heavily during pregnancy. The results are disturbing. A significant number of the infants studied were born with a definite pattern of physical, mental and behavior abnormalities which researchers named the "fetal alcohol syndrome". The babies with this syndrome were shorter and lighter in weight than normal, and didn't "catch up" even after special postnatal care was provided. They also had abnormally small heads, several facial irregularities, joint and limb abnormalities, heart defects, and poor co-ordination. Most also were mentally retarded and showed a number of behavioral problems, including hyperactivity, extreme nervousness, and poor attention spans. Some of the infants were born with all of the characteristics described above, while others showed only some features of the syndrome.

HOW ALCOHOL AFFECTS THE FETUS

It may be hard to believe that alcohol can wreak such devastating effects on the unborn baby. But an understanding of how alcohol interacts with the fetus may help. When a pregnant woman takes a drink, the alcohol readily crosses the placenta to the fetus. Moreover, the alcohol travels through the baby's bloodstream in the same concentration as that of the mother. So, if the expectant mother becomes drunk at a party, her unborn baby becomes drunk as well. But, of course, the tiny, developing system of the fetus is not nearly as equipped to handle alcohol as the system of its adult mother. Among other things, the undeveloped liver of the unborn can burn up alcohol at less than half the rate of the adult liver, which means that alcohol remains in the fetal system longer than in the adult system. Unfortunately, the fetus can't "say" no when it's had enough.

HOW MUCH DRINKING IS HARMFUL?

At present, we don't know exactly how much alcohol, consumed over what period of time, is needed to endanger the developing baby. But based on the research described above as well as on some recently conducted animal studies, it is believed that a pregnant woman clearly risks harm to her baby if she drinks three or more ounces of absolute alcohol per day. Three ounces of absolute alcohol are equivalent to six average-sized drinks. However, we don't know as yet whether levels lower than six drinks per day during pregnancy can also harm the unborn baby. Until now, studies have been limited to the infants of mothers known to drink heavily. Research is currently underway on the effects of moderate drinking on the fetus, to determine whether there is a safe limit for alcohol use during pregnancy. Another unknown, also being investigated, is whether there is a critical period during pregnancy when heavy drinking is most likely to produce the fetal alcohol syndrome.

We also need to know more about the effects on the fetus of episodic, or "binge" drinking. Does a woman who consumes six or more drinks every third Friday night, but abstains in between, still risk harm to her unborn baby? Some preliminary studies show that this kind of drinking pattern may indeed be a factor in development of fetal abnormalities. Since the fetus gets a potent, long-lasting dose of alcohol each time the mother takes a drink, it would not be surprising if further research confirmed the dangers of periodic heavy drinking.

It is important to note that the fetal alcohol syndrome, as far as we know, develops only in response to heavy drinking during pregnancy. There is no evidence so far that alcohol abuse prior to conception endangers the health of the developing baby.

RISK FACTORS

It is well known that many people who abuse alcohol also tend to smoke a lot of cigarettes, use other drugs, pay little attention to nutrition, and generally suffer a great deal of emotional stress. All of these factors are related to reproductive risk. How do we know, then, that alcohol is the real culprit in the development of this pattern of birth abnormalities? Could any of these other behaviors, alone or in combination, be partially or even totally responsible for what we call the fetal alcohol syndrome? At this point, you may feel a little uncertain how to approach drinking during pregnancy. Since not all the research is in yet, there are few hard and fast rules to follow. We do know that if a pregnant woman consumes six or more drinks per day, she clearly risks harm to her unborn baby. But there is much we still don't know about this problem, including the risks of moderate drinking and periodic heavy drinking, whether the fetus is most susceptible to alcohol at a particular time during pregnancy, and whether the fetal alcohol syndrome is related to other risks factors, such as nicotine and poor nutrition. Until all the facts are in, however, it makes sense to exercise caution. As guidelines for alcohol use during pregnancy, you may find the following suggestions useful:

Two Drink Limit

Drink no more than one ounce of absolute alcohol per day. That equals two mixed drinks containing one ounce of liquor each, or two five-ounce glasses of wine, or two twelve-ounce cans of beer. We really don't know at what level alcohol begins to harm the fetus, but there is evidence that a risk is established if you drink six drinks a day or more. Between two and six drinks, the risk factor is uncertain. However, a minimum risk is involved if you limit your drinking to two drinks a day or less.

"Saving Up" Drinks

Two drinks a day means just that. You can't "save" your drinks by, say abstaining for three days during the week, then downing six drinks on a Saturday night party. Remember, your unborn baby achieves the same concentration of alcohol as you do, and retains it in its system for longer than you do. We don't know yet whether one big "night on the town" is enough to cause problems for the fetus. But it's not worth taking the chance.

Don't Switch Drugs

If you are accustomed to coping with tension or depression by having a few drinks, don't fill the void by using other mood-altering drugs, such as tranquilizers or antidepressants. Some of these drugs also may be harmful to the baby when taken during pregnancy, although no proof has yet been established. In fact, since most drugs cross the placental barrier to your baby, it is a good idea to take only those which are absolutely necessary during your pregnancy. Check with your doctor before taking any drugs; including simple over-the-counter medication such as aspirin and sleeping preparations.

Alternatives to Alcohol

Pregnancy changes your life in some important ways, and you are bound to feel some stress during this period. For various reasons, some women experience more anxiety and depression than usual during pregnancy. In any case, there may be times when a few friendly drinks will seem like a good antidote to whatever is troubling you. At those times, stop and try to think of other ways you might handle your feelings.

First, make sure you are clear about just what is bothering you. Is there any specific action you could take to improve the situation? Or would simply talking about your feelings to someone close to you help? Sometimes a long walk, some relaxing music, or some kind of creative outlet can do a lot to relieve stress. Have you ever tried meditation? Writing out your feelings? You may be surprised at how effective some of these alternatives to alcohol can be.

Getting Help

If you find yourself seriously depressed or anxious and can't seem to shake it off, consider getting some outside help. Your local women's center may run a counselling program as well as a number of special support groups for women. Women's centers, area mental health agencies and your own doctor are possible sources for counselling referrals. If you think you may have an alcohol problem, you can find help through your local council on alcoholism, mental health agency, Alcoholics Anonymous chapter, or Women for Sobriety Group. Most of these referral sources can be found in your telephone directory.

You Can Make A Difference

There are lots of "dos" and "don'ts" associated with pregnancy, and sometimes you may feel a bit overwhelmed by them. It often seems there is so much to suspect, reject and avoid! But underlying all the advice and recommendations you receive is the important message that what you do makes a difference. By making informed, intelligent choices about alcohol use during pregnancy, you can increase your chances of bearing a healthy normal baby.

APPENDIX V

AMERICAN INDIANS, NATIVE ALASKANS, AND DRINK

This appendix is extracted from a paper published by the Inter-Tribal Alcoholism Treatment Center in Sheridan, Wyoming, and is reproduced here by permission of the National Institute on Alcohol Abuse and Alcoholism, of the U. S. Department of Health, Education and Welfare. The author is Shirley Robinson, and it is dated 1974.

Most of this paper is devoted to the means then being employed, or suggested for employment, to deal with this problem. Since these are too detailed for this book, and are in some measure out of date, they have been omitted. What follows is, essentially, the over-all background to the problem, which gives some idea of its size. Other and more recent papers have shown that this particular aspect of the problem is, in effect, on the increase in the United States.

Alcoholism and alcohol abuse are not a new problem among American Indians. Historians say that early American frontiersmen, trappers, and traders offered spirituous beverages to Indians as a gesture of friendship. Later, with a different motive, the white man was known to offer alcohol to Indians while treaties and trading rights were being negotiated. Often Indian leaders in a drunken state could be induced to sign away such valuable assets as land and trading rights for next to nothing (Winkler 1968).

Even up to recent times, white men who had been appointed caretakers of Indian affairs were accused of using alcohol as an instrument of control to manipulate Indian people and minimize challenges to their power.

UNDERMINED INDIAN LIFE

Sociologists theorize that because alcohol was virtually unknown to the American native until it was introduced by Europeans, his society had formulated no socially acceptable pattern for dealing with it (Heath 1964). Therefore, its consequences were devastating.

Recognizing that widespread alcohol use was responsible for growing dissension, violence, and poor judgment among Indian people, one chief, Little Turtle, made a direct appeal in 1802 to President Thomas Jefferson for a law or regulation prohibiting liquor sales to Indians (Cohen 1944). Although Mr. Jefferson brought the matter to the attention of Congress that same year, it was not until July 9, 1832 that Congress passed legislation prohibiting liquor traffic to and among Indians. Although the law was passed as a protective measure at the request of the Indian people, it became apparent over the years that it was discriminatory, and it was finally repealed in 1953.

The 1832 law marked the first acknowledgement on the part of the Federal Government that alcohol abuse among Indians is a major social and health problem deserving of National attention. Concern over this problem, however, was until recent years eclipsed by problems of health, housing, sanitation, education and unemployment which overtook the Indians after they were systematically dispossessed of lands and relocated on Federal reservations. The very existence of these problems fostered further use of alcohol, with Indians themselves often considering a state of intoxication a desirable alternative to the harsh realities of life.

In any event, when Federal agencies, the Bureau of Indian Affairs (BIA) and later, the Indian Health Service (IHS), first began assisting the Indians with health and welfare programs they did not give high priority to the problem of alcohol abuse. The two agencies, which are still actively committed to administering programs for the benefit of Indian people, have both added alcoholism efforts in recent years.

However, it was not until the National Institute on Alcohol Abuse and Alcoholism (NIAAA) in a special report to Congress in 1971 named "reducing alcoholism among American Indians" as one of its six priority goals that a concentrated attack supported by substantial revenue was launched by the Federal Government against alcoholism among native Americans.

The new Federal commitment represented by NIAAA money is finally making it possible for alcoholism treatment services to be delivered in many Indian communities—both on the reservation and elsewhere. Years of neglect and festering sociocultural problems such as racial prejudice, deprivation, and educational disadvantage have compounded the problem of alcohol abuse among the estimated 827,000 Indians in this country.

Empirical measures are difficult to apply to Indian drinking habits due to physical isolation, cultural barriers, and resistance by Indians to being studied and surveyed by non-Indians. However, spree drinking and group drinking patterns among Indians have been adequately documented and it is widely conceded that widespread use of alcohol occurs among Indian youth as young as 8 or 9 years of age, especially among Indian boarding school students. While no Indian is anxious to perpetuate the stereotype of "the drunken Indian," an image still widely held by the non-Indian community, tribal leaders and many other concerned Indians describe alcohol abuse as the current number one health problem facing American Indians and their ethnic relatives, the Alaskan natives.

The use of alcohol by Indians is estimated to be double that of the general population and excessive drinking weighs heavily in suicides, homicides, criminal acts, traffic accidents, and acts of violence committed by Indians. A booklet published in 1973 by the National Institute of Mental Health reports that "75 to 80 percent of all suicides among Indians are alcohol related, a rate that exceeds that of the general population two or three times over." In 1972, the National Center for Health Statistics reported the three fastest rising causes of death among Indians, in order of frequency, were cirrhosis of the liver, suicide, and homicide. All three are obviously linked to destructive tendencies and to alcoholism.

ALCOHOL ABUSE NOT ALCOHOLISM

"The damaging effects of alcohol on Indian society are incalculable," according to Bert P. Eder, chief of the NIAAA Indian Desk, which is part of the agency's Division of Special Treatment and Rehabilitation Programs. Mr. Eder, a Sioux from the Ft. Peck Reservation, Mont., said alcohol abuse rather than alcoholism is the big problem among Indians. The rate of alcoholism among Indians closely parallels that of the nation, he said, noting that no proof exists that the physiological reaction of Indians to alcohol is any more severe than that of other racial groups. However, he estimates that well over half of the Indian population uses alcohol consistently and excessively. This large group in turn directly affects the well-being of the total Indian population.

Robert L. Moore, director of the American Indian Commission on Alcoholism and Drug Abuse (AICADA) agreed with this assessment. "There isn't one Indian in this land who isn't affected by alcoholism," he said. AICADA is employed by NIAAA to provide technical assistance to American Indian organizations that administer NIAAA treatment projects. From this vantage point, Mr. Moore and his staff are afforded a first-hand view of alcoholism among Indian people. Mr. Moore, a Seneca Indian from Oklahoma and a graduate of the Federal boarding school system for Indians, says alcohol abuse and alcoholism constitute the "number one killer," and, collectively, the number one health, social, and economic problem among American Indians today.

Drinking problems among Alaskan natives are as bad as, if not worse than, among the Indians, according to Ralph Amouak, a native leader in alcoholism treatment and prevention in Alaska. "We seem to jump from one epidemic to another," he said. "First it was influenza, then tuberculosis; now the health crisis is alcoholism. Where an individual has avoided alcoholism, the likelihood is high that a spouse or family member is alcoholic. Every Alaskan native knows someone or is related to someone who drank himself to death." Mr. Amouak is an advisor with the Alaska Native Commission on Alcoholism and Drug Abuse.

It is generally agreed that there is an urgent need for effective treatment services for Indian alcoholism, but NIAAA officials recognize that the need will not be met unless Indians play a role in the process. Therefore, the Institute has made Indian participation in planning, development, and implementation a fundamental requirement of the Indian projects it funds. "We can't hope the program will succeed unless Indian sociocultural expectations are taken into account. The only way to do that is to insist the programs be intrinsically Indian from the start," Mr. Eder said.

BIBLIOGRAPHY

This should be more accurately entitled "substitute for a bibliography," since I am not a doctor and do not pretend to have read a fraction of the vast amount—much of it erroneous—that has been published over the centuries on both the psychological and the somatic aspects of the disease called alcoholism. For a medical examination of both aspects, I would refer the reader to *The Disease Concept of Alcoholism*, by Professor E. M. Jellinek, published by the College and University Press, New Haven, Connecticut, in association with the Hillhouse Press, New Brunswick, New Jersey. The first edition appeared in October 1960, but has been updated in later editions. His Appendix C, combined with his bibliography, must run to well over five hundred volumes, papers, etc. As greater attempts than ever before are being made now to understand the nature of this strange disease (recently described by the World Health Organization as the third greatest killer on a global scale) and, if possible, to discover better methods toward a cure or at least a retardation of its progressive nature, any medical bibliography must rapidly become out of date. Those organizations known to this author, which may respond to any questions on any aspects of the disease are:

The Christopher D. Smithers Center, 410 West Fifty-eighth, New York City, N.Y. 10019.

The National Clearing House for Alcohol Information, P.O. Box 2345, Rockville, Md. 20852.

The British Medical Association, Tavistock Square, London WC1.

The Irish National Council on Alcoholism, 19 Fleet Street, Dublin 2.

If not themselves in possession of any technical or specialized information required, any of these organizations should be able to say where such information is available.

For the rest I have usually given the source of my information, if written, in the text of the book. However, in the matter of American temperance movements, culminating in prohibition, I have also drawn on *Ardent Spirits*, by John Kobler, Putnam, New York, 1973. In dealing with Alcoholics Anonymous, I have relied largely, and with acknowledgments in this text, on the Ninth (English) printing of

Marty Mann's *Primer on Alcoholism*, Victor Gollancz, Ltd., London, 1974. Again, the various branches of AA, to be found in most telephone directories, can be of help to the man or woman who would know more, particularly concerning that organization.

INDEX

Aborigines (Australia), 26
Abortion, 106
Accidents, road, alcoholism and, 169–83
Addiction, 20–24
Adler, Alfred, 95, 96, 126
Alanon, 161–62
Alaskans (native), 191–94
Alcohol, 16–19
  Alaskans (native) and, 191–94
  cancer and, 24
  ethyl, 99
  history of, 25–27, 41–46
  international per capita
    consumption of, 183–84
  medical uses of, 23
  methyl, 16
  pregnancy and, 106, 185–90
  Red Indians and, 191–94
  as a sedative drug, 18–19, 24
  taxes on, 18–19
Alcoholic poisoning, 44
Alcoholics
  defined, 99
  endogenous, 27
  five main types of, 100–1
  percentage of all drinkers who
    become, 100, 103–4
  women versus men, 105
Alcoholics Anonymous, 79, 94, 155, 161–62
Alcoholism, 22–23
  Antabuse and, 122, 145, 159–60, 162
  crucial phase, symptoms of, 131–34, 152–53
  definition of, 27

as a disease, 93–94
environment and, 28–29, 67–68
in general hospitals, 177–78
heredity and, 2, 28, 30, 99, 105
India and, 91, 93
the industrial worker and, 163–68
  programs to aid, 165–66
modern literature on, 3–4
prodromal phase, 2, 99
  four principal symptoms of, 123
Prohibition and, 90
psychoanalysis and, 94–98
psychological help for, 161–62
as psychosomatic, 102, 157
road accidents and, 169–83
secret drinking, 38–40
steps required for curing, 153–54
symptoms of, 34–35
U.S.S.R. and, 29, 68
ways to reach disease stage, 27–28
Alexander the Great, 101
Alpha alcoholics, 100
American Indian Commission on
  Alcoholism and Drug Abuse
  (AICADA), 193, 194
American Indians, see Red Indians
Americans, The (Furnas), 75–84
American Temperance Society, 70, 75–76, 77
American Temperance Union, 77
Amish, 71
Antabuse, 122, 145, 159–60, 162
Anti-Saloon League, 86–87
Arabian Bird, The (FitzGibbon), 115
Armagnac, 44
Arthur, T. S., 77

Australia, licensing laws, 66

Baptists, 42, 73
Beecher, Dr. Lyman, 76
Beer, 42–43, 68
Bell, Clive, 11
Beta alcoholics, 100
Bible, the, 26–27, 76
Blackouts, 123, 124–26
Bootleggers, 90–91
Bottle, The (play), 81
Bradley, General Omar, 15
Brandy, 43
Bureau of Indian Affairs (BIA), 192
Byron, George Gordon, 31

Calvados, 18
Calvin, John, 70, 72
Calvinism, 72, 73
Cancer, 22
  alcohol and, 24
  cigarettes and, 20
  lung, 20
Cannabis, 17–19, 113
Capone, Al, 90
Central Intelligence Agency (CIA), 115
Chesterton, G. K., 57
Childhood, drinking and, 105–14
Chinese gin, 44
Christianity, 41–42, 70
Christian Science, 42
Churchill, Winston, 36, 55, 101
Cigarettes, 21–22
  cancer and, 20
Cigars, 22
Cirrhosis of the liver, 110
Clare, Dr. Anthony W., 169n
Clark, Billy James, 75, 78
Cocaine, 17, 113
Cognac, 44
Cold Water Army, 80
Collier, Constance, 142
Confucianism, 42, 70, 93
Cooney, Dr. John G., 145, 146, 148, 158–59, 162, 169n
Crack-up, The (Fitzgerald), 3
Cruikshank, George, 81

Dante, 98

Darwin, Charles, 67
Davenport, John, 14
Defence of the Realm Act (DORA), 88
De Gaulle, Charles, 110
Delirium tremens (DTs), 148, 149, 160
Delta alcoholics, 101
Dent, Dr., 121, 122, 135, 160
Depression, 31–33, 161
  climate and, 67–68
  endogenous, 31–34, 66–67, 69
  Jekyll and Hyde syndrome, 32–33
  reactive, 31, 33, 67, 69
Deserted Village (Goldsmith), 56
De Valera, Eamon, 146
Diabetes, 24, 36, 135, 147–48
Douglas, Norman, 41, 118–20
Drugs, 22, 99, 112–13
Drunkard, The (play), 81

Edwards, Jonathan, 72
Elder, Duke, 134–35
Electra complex, 95
Elegy Written in a Country Churchyard (Gray), 56
Endogenous alcoholic, 27
Endogenous depression, 31–32, 66–67, 69
Environment, 28–29, 67–68
Epsilon alcoholics, 101, 142
Ethyl alcohol, 99
Euphoria, postalcoholic, 157–58

Far from the Madding Crowd (Hardy), 56
Fermented mare's milk, 43
Fitzgerald, F. Scott, 3
FitzGibbon, Constantine
  alcoholic collapse of, 149–51
  awarded Guggenheim Fellowship, 134
  blackouts of, 147
  books written by, 115, 117, 120, 125, 128–30, 146, 148–49, 150, 158
  childhood of, 7–8
  depressions of, 7–8, 117, 148, 149
  diabetes, 135, 147–48
  Douglas and, 118–20